Tim Smith is one of America's key authorities on the teen years, and *Almost Cool* will put your heart in touch with the incredible needs of adolescents. This book is insightful and practical.

Jim Burns
President, National Institute of Youth Ministry

Tim Smith has not only a refreshingly positive take on teenagers, but he understands the unique challenges of being a parent. *Almost Cool* provides the kind of practical help and encouragement every parent needs.

Wayne Rice
Director, Understanding Your Teenager seminars

This book is loaded with practical wisdom, but it is not heavy, and each chapter is sprinkled liberally with humor. It's like having the medicine—we parents need it, and it's easy to swallow. Well-read and a veteran youth worker, Tim Smith knows what he's talking about.

Dave Veerman
Author, Parenting Passages

Almost Cool

YOU *CAN* FIGURE OUT HOW TO PARENT YOUR TEEN

Almost Cool

TIM SMITH

MOODY PRESS
CHICAGO

© 1997 by
TIM D. SMITH

All Scripture quotations, unless indicated, are taken from the *Holy Bible: New International Version*®. NIV®. Copyright © 1973, 1978, 1984 by International Bible Society. Used by permission of Zondervan Publishing House. All rights reserved.

The "NIV" and "New International Version" trademarks are registered in the United States Patent and Trademark Office by International Bible Society. Use of either trademark requires permission of International Bible Society.

ISBN: 0-8024-6391-6

1 3 5 7 9 10 8 6 4 2

Printed in the United States of America

To the thousands of "cool" parents
I have had the privilege
of serving since 1973

CONTENTS

CHARTS ABOUT TEENS

Chapter 1
UNDERSTAND THEIR WORLD

Our children change a lot when they leave behind their toys for the teenage years. That was then; this is now:

She used to leave her Barbies all over the bathroom floor;
    now she leaves foundation, eye-liner, and lipstick.

He used to play with cars and make noises with his mouth;
    now he drives a car and makes noises with his foot.

She used to take bubble baths;
    now she takes an hour.

He loved to play army;
    soon he might join.

She used to talk on the phone to Grandma for three minutes;
    now she talks for hours, but not to Grandma.

He cleaned up his room in five minutes, stuffing his toy chest;
>   now he cleans it in five minutes, stuffing his closet.

The refrigerator door used to be for magnets and art projects;
>   now it is open more than it is closed.

She used to want to be dropped off at the school door;
>   now she requests a block away.

He grew up with Power Rangers and video games;
>   now he toys with power processors, CD-ROM, and websites.

She used to spend hours on the floor;
>   now she spends hours on the floor of the mall.

"Where are you going?" "Outside," he would always say;
>   now, "Where are you going?" "Nowhere," comes the reply.

She used to snuggle just for how it felt;
>   now she snuggles when she needs money.

He was convinced you knew everything;
>   now he is convinced you know nothing.

She used to walk with her hand in yours;
>   now she wants to walk on the other side of the street.

He used to watch you shave and drive;
>   now he drives and has redefined "close shave."

Dust off the photo albums and pause to reflect,
>   your little girl and boy are growing up.

Take a deep breath and ignore the phone,
>   admit it—you have a teenager at home!

Many adults are nervous about teenagers. They see them talking loud and acting obnoxious in a public place. Teens use language and wear clothes that seem inappropriate. Their music is too loud and too weird. But what really makes parents anxious is seeing their precious, innocent children approach adolescence.

Will my son walk to school looking like that?

Could they just take in my daughter at the convent?

"It was the best of times, it was the worst of times." This is what parents tell me about their own teenage years. Being a teenager is an emotional and confusing stage of life.

Parenting teens is emotional and confusing too! Perhaps it has never been more difficult than it is now. Because of the changes in our culture and families, and because of all the risks that teens are exposed to, we wonder, *How do we parent?*

Don't panic! I have good news. This may be the best time to be raising teenagers. Sure, it is difficult, but we have more resources, tools, and support than our parents did. Hopefully, we will be able to effectively parent our teens, and still do it differently from our parents.

When I was fifteen, one of my primary concerns was driving. Now, at fifteen, many teens are worried about drive-bys (shootings). Yes, it is a different world. Let's see if we can understand it. If we can see some of the issues in their world, it will help us understand our teenager.

MEET GENERATION V

In my work with teens and families I have noticed a change in the last few years. Teens and parents are thinking about values. The term *family values* has become a political football recently, but in reality, values are something Americans *are* thinking about. Though our teenagers represent the younger end of what has been called Generation X, *Parade* magazine has called them Generation V for their desire for stronger moral values:

One could think of them as Generation "V"—for values. According to The Mood of American Youth study, today's teens are neither as rebellious as adolescents in the 1970's nor as materialistic as those of the 1980's. What they want is not to change the world or to own a chunk of it, but to be happy. Among the teens' greatest concerns: the decline in moral and social values.[1]

The writer referred to a 1996 survey, conducted by NFO Research, Inc., that polled 938 young people aged thirteen to seventeen who were representative of America's adolescent population as a whole. "Of those polled, nine teens in ten say they don't drink or smoke. Seven in ten say religion is important in their lives. And six in ten—boys as well as girls—don't approve of premarital sex."[2]

This is good news. Sometimes it's helpful to see that not all teens are on the greased slide to destruction. Not all teens are automatic victims of negative peer pressure. Let's not sell them short. The majority of teens are sensible and caring. Of course, most of the time, these kids don't make the papers. It reminds me of a saying by contemporary Christian music pioneer Larry Norman. When asked why he was playing, "Christian rock," he replied, "Why should the devil have all of the good music?"

My question is, "Why should the devil get all the media about how 'bad' teens are these days?"

I believe kids have not been fairly represented. They have been labeled, "slackers" and "self-indulged." Sure, some are, but many are trying to make a difference and make a better world.

In fact, most teens today assimilate their parents' values. According to the survey,

Most of the respondents respect their parents, get along well with them and consider their rules strict but fair. . . . Today's kids want to have successful careers, but they know that, without family and love, they wouldn't be satisfied. . . . The generation gap seems to have shrunk to a gully. Nearly nine in ten teens (89%) say their parents are interested in their concerns, and 75 percent say *their* parents understand their problems.[3]

I know what you are thinking: *I am living with the 11 percent who think parents are hopelessly out of it!*

Maybe you are, but don't throw in the parenting towel. I promise to send help. One of the most common mistakes parents make is assuming they have lost their influence with their child, simply because she is now a teenager. You can actually influence your teenager.

WATCH YOUR ACTIVE TEENAGER

The first step in influencing your teen is understanding the world she lives in.

To help you, remember the word ACTIVE. In my research and observation, I have noticed that teens live in a world that can be described with six words that spell an acronym: *Active.*

I like acronyms. They help us remember key points. As a parent of a teenager you will appreciate anything that helps your memory and keeps things simple.

The world of our teenagers is ACTIVE: They are *ambivalent* and full of *change* and *technology,* as they seek *independence,* explore *values,* and become more *emotional.*

A—Ambivalent

Adolescents live in an ambivalent world. Sometimes they feel like children; sometimes they feel like adults. Sometimes they want to be left alone; other times they want our direction. They live in a blurry world, which makes things hard for us parents.

It is ambivalent being a parent of a teenager; it is even more so to be a teenager. Once, certain things were limited to the adult world. Our children were restricted from things that might harm them: certain pictures, activities, and conversations. Now that notion seems "discriminatory." Television and the computer world of the Internet, for all their good information, expose our teens earlier to topics that blur the lines between childhood and adulthood.

Some teens may not want to grow up. They have seen what happens to adults and they want no part of it. But, for some of us, we can't take the time to comprehend such "childishness." We want our teens to grow up in a hurry. We don't have the time to protect them from all the worries of the adult world. We aren't comfortable with this no-man's-land of adolescence, so we rush our kids through it.

There is a trend in our culture to treat teens like adults, to minimize the differences between the two. When we reduce the natural boundary that separates childhood from adulthood, we rush our kids into situations they are not equipped to handle. They are no longer protected, but hurried.

With such information given early, teens typically feel ambivalent. They may be excited about their future and worry about it at the same time. Meanwhile they are looking for role models to set the pace, but often are disappointed by those they look up to. Teens' heroes decades ago were people they could admire. Teens still pay attention to heroes, but now their heroes often are the flawed celebrities of entertainment and sports. Indeed, the well-known are often notorious.

Teens live in a world of optimism and disappointment. They live in a world that is ambivalent.

C—Change

Probably one of the best words to describe adolescence is *change*. Teens face changes physically, sexually, emotionally, intellectually, and socially. The word *adolescence* means "the period of growth to maturity." Doesn't that sound comforting? Take a break, get yourself a Diet Pepsi, and ponder that definition.

"Adolescence is the period of growth to maturity."

This is encouraging, even hopeful. The word *period* implies that this stage won't last forever. And I like the idea of *growth*. In fact, a rush of anticipation comes over me when I think about my teens growing to *maturity!*

Of course, this all involves change. The wise parent understands that his teen is going through a period of tremendous change. He understands this and accepts it; in fact he welcomes it. Instead of being ambushed by the changes and challenges of adolescence, a parent can help his teen prepare for them.

T—*Technology*

The world of the teenager is increasingly technological. We all know that if we need help with a technological device we should just ask a teenager.

I remember when I used my video camera for the first time. I wanted to tape a junior high event at church, but I was having difficulty installing the AC adapter. I tried several ways. I read the manual. I tried muscling it. I had been struggling with it for ten minutes, when a junior high student came up and said, "Here, it goes on this way," and snapped it in place. It took him two seconds!

Teens are comfortable with most technological advances: video players, video games, computers, and much more. Most of them have had digital watches since they were seven years old. They can program a VCR, actually use the special effects on a video camera, and find their way around the Internet. Many teens have programmable CD players in their rooms, along with phones with speed dials—linking them to their friends in seconds. They live and play in a world of technology.

Technology offers a user-friendly world, free of instructions and accountability. For instance, can you imagine your image emerging from the video game screen, with your finger pointing at your teen after an hour of play, and your voice saying, "You have had enough video games; now turn this off and do your homework!"?

It won't happen. But it's a good idea.

Technology is largely value-free. If you don't believe me, hop on the Internet for a romp through all kinds of bizarre and unprincipled information. This is the world of our teenagers. Once again, it is ambivalent. Having the technology is useful, but there is a downside to it as well.

I—Independence

Teens live in a world where they are seeking to be more independent. With most mothers working, teens are growing up with less supervision. Sometimes, the freedom gets them into trouble. "Young people today, for example, are freer than ever before to engage in sexual activity, to abuse drugs, and to flout adult authority. At the same time, they are less prepared than ever before to manage these new freedoms."[4]

Our culture has given youth unbridled opportunities. For some, they have taken advantage of the situation. For others, the freedom has led to self-destructive behavior.

But the same thing is true of their parents. In the spirit of independence, some parents have chosen divorce as a way to "meet my own needs" and "get into healthier relationships." Teens notice their parents' pursuit of autonomy and happiness. It is something they want for themselves. For the teens and the parents, the pursuit of independence may be a stronger influence than keeping the family together and close.

Our culture values independence; it is part of our heritage. Mary Pipher, Ph.D., author of the bestseller *Reviving Ophelia,* discusses independence's effect on families:

> The great respect that Americans have for independence creates certain difficulties in families. . . . Our nation began with a Declaration and a War of Independence. We admire feisty individualists, and our heroes are explorers, pioneers, and iconoclasts. . . . The freedom that we value in our culture we also value in our families. Americans believe adolescence is

the time when children emotionally separate from their parents, and this assumption becomes a self-fulfilling prophecy. Daughters behave as they are expected to behave, and ironically, if they are expected to rebel, they will rebel. They distance from their parents, criticize parental behavior, reject parental information and keep secrets. . . . Parents are fearful and angry when their daughters take enormous risks to prove they are independent.[5]

The teenage years are when our kids want to be left alone to make their own choices. For many of them, the sheer number of choices is overwhelming.

Remember growing up? We had three choices of television—the three networks: ABC, the Always Boring Channel; NBC, the Never Believable Channel; and CBS, Continually Bland Stuff. Usually, nothing was on that was of any interest to kids. Now, kids can have hundreds of choices with cable or satellite service. They can be overwhelmed with just the choices of entertainment. The same goes for movies. There used to be one movie theater in many towns. Now we have complexes with twelve or more selections at one time!

Teens today face bewildering choices. They have been given more freedom to choose. But they are often no better prepared to make their decisions than you or I were as teenagers. Sometimes independence feels like abandonment.

V—Value Exploration

Teens are learning about values. I know what you are thinking; you don't believe your teen ever thinks about values. I know it can seem strange, but our teens do. They just don't want us to know.

Actually, teens spend a lot of time thinking about values. They would call it, "Stuff that is important to me." Adolescence is a time to explore values. The average teen may take a big chunk of his life to explore a value. For instance, a sophomore might take one whole month of his sophomore year to consider the value of being polite. Of course, this has a point.

He is trying to get his act together to ask a cute girl to home-coming.

Teens will often try on various "hats" as they explore their identity. Along with the new test-drive of identity often goes a new set of values. For instance, I have actually seen high school students change their social groups, wardrobe, and values three or four times in one school year.

Richard came into his sophomore year with a renewed determination to meet new friends. His freshman year was a "disaster." His sophomore year was going to be different. He joined the marching band and hung around with the band members at lunch. He noticed that the guys in the band wore a certain type of pants—kind of like the Toughskins you used to get at Sears. He talked his mom into buying some. He also noticed that they weren't too concerned about sports and the popular kids at school. They were a culture unto themselves. After all, "they knew music, and the others didn't."

Marching band season ended when football ended. Richard wasn't sure what would happen next. Most of his band friends were going to play in the Stage Band, a special jazz band students had to audition for. He was afraid to try out. Instead, he decided to try out for the wrestling team. He made the team (though his band friends now teased him about being a "jock"). He traded his Toughskin pants for Levis 501's, the required uniform for the athletes. He started wearing a baseball cap, backwards, and developed a jock's swagger. He didn't hang out with the band "geeks" anymore. He was, after all, an athlete. He had a reputation to maintain. At lunch, he sat in the quad and made fun of the nerds and geeks.

He didn't do that well at wrestling, even though he made new friends. It helped his self-esteem. But he still wasn't cool. At his school, wrestling wasn't the coolest sport—surfing was. He decided to try his luck. One of the guys in his biology class took him after school. He was hooked. He bought a surfboard, bleached his hair, and let it grow out. He wore flannel shirts and shorts and sandals. He definitely was not a jock anymore. Now he was a cool surfer.

Richard went through a radical transformation that year. He changed his peer group, his look, his activities and his values three times in six months. At the beginning of his sophomore year, Richard valued quiet conformity and security. As the year progressed, he became more concerned with being noticed and becoming popular. Eventually, his most important ambition was to be cool. Richard was trying on the various "hats" that high school had to offer.

Teenagers are sampling from a menu of values as they seek to develop their identity. They explore values as a group. They observe behavior and consider how consistent it is with expressed values. As they explore new values, teens desperately desire the company of a close friend. The influence of a peer can shape or reinforce a teen's values.

E—Emotional

Teenagers can be very emotional. You have noticed, haven't you? They may look like adults, but teenagers can think and act like children, adolescents, or adults. At any one time, you don't know if you are dealing with the child, the adolescent, or the adult.

Teens can trap themselves in their own emotional web. They may create an imaginary audience for themselves, as if they were onstage. They may feel that others are thinking and talking about them. Others are discussing their clothes, complexion, and companions. Teenagers sometimes believe that everyone else is always thinking about what they are thinking about—them!

This is important for parents to understand. In fact, it can explain a lot of teenage behavior. "The need to play to the imaginary audience helps to explain the extreme self-consciousness of adolescents. But at the same time, teens *want* to be looked at and thought about, because that confirms their sense of self-worth."[6]

23

With all of this introspection, teens are quite melodramatic at times. They are riding an emotional roller coaster. There are thrills and screams of laughter followed by intense moments of fear and a gasp for breath.

This is the world of the teenager, an exciting and sometimes frightening world. It's a world that is constantly changing and seldom predictable. People who claim to have teenagers all figured out obviously aren't parents of teenagers.

The first step in helping our teens ride the roller coaster of adolescence is to understand that world. There are many changes, twists, and turns in their world, but some things have remained constant over the years. Read the following statement and guess who said it, and when: "I see no hope for the future of our people if they are dependent on the frivolous youth of today, for certainly all youth are reckless beyond words. . . . When I was a boy, we were taught to be discreet and respectful of elders, but the present youth are exceedingly wise and impatient of restraint."

Who made that comment about contemporary teenagers? Ronald Reagan in the '80s? Dwight Eisenhower in the '50s? Bill Clinton in the '90s? No, it wasn't any of these modern Americans. The quote is from the eighth century Greek historian Hesiod. Seems that the more things change, the more they stay the same.

For "Almost Cool" Parents

"For 'Almost Cool' Parents" appears at the end of each chapter to help you review and think about key ideas in the chapter. The five questions invite discussion, so I invite you to dialogue with your spouse or a group of other parents. These questions are ideal for discussion in a Sunday school class or small group study. Such dialogue and reflection can help you along the path to becoming "almost cool" parents.

1. What makes parents nervous about teenagers?
2. Do you agree that there is a trend in our culture to treat teens like adults?
3. Have you observed a teen like Richard exploring values and experimenting with social groups?
4. Hesiod's quote is an observation about youth that seems to be universal. How can it be that today's teens seem to be dealing with similar issues as those the youth of Hesiod's day faced?
5. Why is it important to understand the world of our teenagers?

Chapter 2
UNDERSTAND YOUR TEEN

Teens often hear adults say, "These are the best years of your life, enjoy them." No wonder our kids have a difficult time believing us. They are thinking, *My dad must really have a sad life if his teenage years were the* best *years!*

Probably one of the greatest myths we could perpetuate is the one about how great growing up is. We who have survived adolescence should know better. Remember the years of anxiety about the way we look, the stress about failing, the uncertainty about our friends accepting us, and our parents staying together? Ah, yes—those were the good ol' days! Being a teenager is like being on a roller coaster and wanting to get off because you are sick, but everyone keeps telling you what a thrilling ride you are having.

Not too long ago our family made the obligatory trip to The Amusement Park. My kids talked me into going on one of those sadistic roller coasters. You know the type. The kind that threatens to kill you by either breaking your neck with whiplash or causing cardiac arrest in the middle of your third backward loop. I survived the first round of the torture and stumbled to a bench. My kids skipped back for another turn. My head eventually stopped ringing. I could begin to focus my eyes.

I was sitting at the bottom of a steep ramp. I watched the top of the ramp, where people emerged from the roller coaster. Smiling, polyester-wearing attendants guided the riders toward the exit ramp. "This way to exit, sir," they said, pointing and smiling sadistically. "Please exit the cars and follow the yellow arrow down the ramp, ma'am." People followed their instructions like they were drugged. Mesmerized by the trauma of the ride, they stumbled toward the top of the ramp; then gravity took over. I'd like to know who designs these places. Why do they have a ramp slanted down at a forty-five degree angle at the ride's exit? Isn't the ride scary enough?

Being the ever-alert observer of human nature (and nursing a throbbing headache) I decided to watch more closely the people coming down the ramp. There were basically two types of roller coaster survivors: (1) those who happily skipped down the steep ramp, smiling and looking normal; and (2) those who couldn't brace themselves against the gravity and were pulled down, grabbing at the rails, friends, strangers, anything to support themselves. Being a teenager is like that. Sometimes your teen can look cool and walk like she is in total control. Other times she will be out of control and feel like a complete derelict. (At times she may even look like one.)

THE NEGATIVES—AND POSITIVES—OF ADOLESCENCE

I think some of us, as parents, have a prejudicial view of adolescence. We talk about all the "peer pressure." We, of course, are thinking about negative peer pressure. Peer pressure —the influence of friends, largely determined by expectations and fears—can also be positive. Positive peer pressure happened when Christa invited Shawna to learn how to make jewelry. Shawna had been spending many of her afternoons after school drinking and getting into trouble with guys. She had become sexually active. Christa saw this and suggested they get together and make some earrings. Shawna enjoyed her time with Christa and immersed herself in their new hobby. As they worked, Christa was able to talk with her friend about Shawna's rocky, unsatisfactory times with guys. Because of Christa's support, Shawna agreed to get help. They called me.

Positive peer pressure means encouraging a friend to go out for a sport when she is afraid to. It is organizing a study group to prepare for a test. It is helping someone finish his chores at home so he can go out with friends. Don't sell your child short; she can be a positive influence on other teens. Indeed, positive peer pressure can be just as strong as negative peer pressure.

I like what Temple University professor Laurence Steinberg says about adolescence: "Adolescence is not an inherently difficult period. The evils of peer pressure have been overrated. The decline of the family has been overstated."[1] Steinberg reports that being a teenager doesn't mean your son or daughter will have any more problems than in any other stage of life. According to his research, nearly 90 percent of teenagers avoid serious trouble.[2] That's good news!

So why do some adults say adolescence is tough? Maybe it isn't any different from other stages of life, but maybe it *feels* that way. Maybe teens don't have the skills to process the challenges of life; it feels so intense, and at times, overwhelming. Maybe they don't have the verbal skills to talk about their feelings. In his research, Steinberg has discovered some encouraging findings. Divorce, economics, the media, violence, and dysfunction have all taken their toll on the family, but most parents remain the major influence on their children through adolescence and into young adulthood. The parent's example and involvement and the home environment (which is determined mainly by the parent) even influence a child's interest and performance in school.[3]

WHAT TEENS WANT

As parents we *do* have the main influence on our teens. If we can understand them better, we can help them mature into independent and responsible adults. This means, in part, understanding what teens want. I am not saying we need to give in to their whims and cater to their wishes. I am asking, "What does your teen want out of life?" and "Do you have a strategy to assist your teen in reaching his goals in life?" The first step is to discover what most teens desire in their lives. The 1996 NFO Research survey of 938 teens mentioned in chapter 1 also asked teens to list their goals in life. Chart 1 shows what the researchers found:[4]

Chart 1 **TOP TWELVE THINGS** **TEENS WANT MOST FROM LIFE:**
1. Happiness 2. Long/enjoyable life 3. Marriage/family 4. Financial success 5. Career success 6. Religious satisfaction 7. Love 8. Personal success 9. Personal contribution to society 10. Friends 11. Health 12. Education

Take another look at the results. Encouraging, aren't they? What would you have said kids want? A pile of money? To be a celebrity? To rule the Free World? Based on the survey results, these teenagers' aspirations are admirable. For the Christian parent, we would like to see religious satisfaction be higher in the results, but it is notable that it even made the list; considering this was a representative sample of teens in our country—those who attend church and those who don't.

WHAT TEENS THINK

The researchers also asked teens their opinions on contemporary issues. The following findings show our teens are fairly sensible and conservative. (The survey is accurate to within plus or minus 3 percentage points.):[5]

Chart 2 TEENS' VIEWS ON CONTEMPORARY ISSUES	
Families and Children	**Agree**
Teenagers are not prepared to have babies	91%
A single parent can raise a family	75%
I am very likely to raise my children differently than I was raised	55%
Abortion should remain legal	48%
Premarital sex is okay	40%
In the Schools	
Condoms should be available in schools	61%
Local school officials should be able to censor books	47%
School prayer should not be permitted	32%
Sex education should be done by parents, not in schools	32%

Surveys are helpful because they give us insight into teenagers. They can help us begin to understand what might be going on inside our teen's head. The results of this survey reflect a fairly conservative teenage population. Teenagers may wear weird clothes and listen to annoying music, but a large percentage of them has views and values we would endorse.

In case you haven't noticed, teenagers like to share their opinions. Help develop your teen's mental abilities by asking him what he thinks. You could use these survey results to stimulate dialogue with your teen. As teens talk about their opinions, they are challenged to think deeper about them. They are forced to exercise some mental muscle, and they don't even have to sweat! This is one subtle way you can help your teen sharpen his logic—ask his opinion on an issue.

WHAT TEENS FEEL

Teens live in a world of change. Some handle it better than others. Change can be stressful, especially if it catches a person unprepared. A wise parent prepares his teen by explaining the changes, including the deluge of emotions that are part of adolescence.

I know parents who have prepared a list of emotions that they anticipated their teen would experience. Before their child hit the adolescent storm, they shared the list with him or her. They dated it and filed it away until their teen began to demonstrate the whirlwind of emotions. They then pulled out the list, discussed it with their teen, and tried to stay reasonable. "These are normal emotions for teenagers. You are not weird," they comforted their son or daughter. "Remember, we told you that some day you may feel this way. See, it's right here in our handwriting and dated two years ago.

"The problem isn't you or us; it is this particular stage of life you have to go through. It is temporary. You can make it. We will be here for you."

The parents have told me that this simple list helped them keep their wits and gave their teenagers hope. Consider using the following list with your teen or preteen.[6]

Chart 3
FEELINGS TEENS MAY EXPERIENCE

1. Nobody likes me . . . especially Mom and/or Dad.
2. I feel ugly.
3. Nobody understands or cares.
4. Any place would be better than here.
5. I feel like running away from home.
6. I just wish everyone would leave me alone!
7. My parents treat me like such a baby.
8. I feel like crying all the time.
9. Sometimes I feel like I am going crazy.
10. Everyone is looking at me.

WHAT TEENS NEED

We have discussed what our teens want out of life, and what they think and feel; but what do teens *need*? Remember what we said about adolescence? "Adolescence is a period of *growth* to maturity." Notice the word *growth*. Teens are going through a stage of rapid growth. As these changes hit them, they are confronted with a variety of tasks necessary to adapt to the growth. These tasks are called *developmental tasks*—tasks that teens need to be able to do if they are going to grow and develop. Teens face changes physically, sexually, emotionally, intellectually, and socially. The wise parent anticipates these and helps her teen walk through them.

The wise parent is not sidetracked by the externals: your daughter may look like a model; your son might be able to slam-dunk; and their rooms might look like biology experiments. It does not matter. The wise parent focuses on the internals (rather than the externals) to deal with the change and challenges of each stage of life. Change is an inevitable part of life. Adolescence is a time of change for both the child and the parent.

Sometimes the challenge of change can lead to conflict.

Parents might be asking midlife identity questions at the same time their teen is seeking a sense of self. Parents are realizing that their bodies and careers have limits. Teens are waking up to new and broader horizons. "The adolescent's spurt often collides with his parent's midlife reassessment—that critical time in life when marriages, careers, life pursuits, values and priorities are questioned, turned around and drastically altered."[7]

Parents and teens face common life-stage issues at the same time. Often though, they are heading in opposite directions. Physically teens are becoming stronger and bigger, while many parents are becoming weaker and rounder. In terms of careers, teens are beginning to think about vocational preparation, including possible college, and may be working part-time; parents are wondering about abilities that have peaked, job satisfaction, and are saving for retirement.

And what about emotions? Teens can be impulsive and self-centered, but parents often are struggling with feelings too. "The teenager's frequent need for immediate gratification seems to be a left-over childhood tendency simply not yet outgrown."[8] Teens don't want to wait. But some midlife adults can be this way too. We have all seen grown men go out and buy a red convertible and don trendy clothes, excessive jewelry, and a cavalier attitude. They are in *search of themselves.* Teens often have similar journeys. Your teenager may be more like you than you thought.

PERSONAL CHANGES AND HELPING OUR TEENS

Have you ever asked yourself, "How do my life-stage issues and my teen's issues impact each other?" You may be experiencing some of the same issues and challenges as your teenager. I believe it is by design. At a time when our teens need us to be available for support, we often are hit with our own adolescent-like issues. I think God designed it that way to make us more sensitive and understanding. As the apostle Paul wrote, "The Father of compassion and the God of all comfort . . . comforts us in all our troubles, so that we can comfort those in any trouble with the comfort we ourselves have received from God" (2 Corinthians 1:3).

In working with youth, I have discovered that it is easier to relate to teens if I have gone through a similar situation. I'm not as quick with solutions, but I tend to take more time to understand and interact. This seems to work well with teenagers. I have even tried it on our adolescent daughters. Of course, it is easier to experiment on other people's kids. If it doesn't work, you don't have to live with them.

Our Pain, Their Pain

Notice in the verse above that God comforts us. This means we are in pain. As parents it is helpful to admit to ourselves, and to our teens, that we sometimes face trouble. We should admit that we are vulnerable to pain. When we relate as authentic human beings, people who cry and hurt, we build bridges into the lives of our teens. When we are real we build bridges because we and our teen are on the same level. If we always try to relate as a perfect parent who has no troubles; we are relating down instead of across. Relating down tends to build barriers, relating across tends to build bridges.

Which do you want to build into your relationship with your teenager—bridges or barriers? "Seek first to understand, then to be understood," Stephen Covey has written.[9] Instead of demanding that our teens understand us and see it our way, it is helpful to take time to understand them. This doesn't mean we give in and become wimpy, permissive parents. It does mean that we show respect, humility, and authenticity to our teens by taking the time to understand them.

Communication is primarily seeking to be understood. If we can create an environment of understanding, our teens will be more likely to talk with us. A slogan that I try to remember when I am seeking to understand teens is, "Connect first, direct second." If your teen feels like you have connected with her, she is more likely to take direction from you. If she doesn't feel that you have connected with her and understood her, she will be resistant to any attempts to guide her.

Humility and Compassion

Seeking to understand first requires us as parents to be humble. It demonstrates that we value our teen and their opinion. We may not agree with their opinions, but we value them enough to try to understand them.

Contrast this with the parent who is convinced he is right. He doesn't really want his teenager's opinions. He wants submission. He wants cooperation. He wants his teen to live up to his expectations and agree with his opinions. His motto is: "If I wanted your opinion, I would give it to you!"

Such arrogance is so unlike God. As our heavenly Father, God doesn't have to exercise His authority to understand us and relate to us. He doesn't allow His authority to interfere in the relationship. Instead, He is a "Father of compassion." The word *compassion* means "to feel with" another and comes from two root words, *com* meaning "with," and *passion* meaning "a strong liking or desire." Similar to *empathy*, *compassion* means, "sympathetic awareness of others' distress, together with a desire to alleviate it." When a father shows such compassion, he becomes a powerful example of God.

Compassion involves listening. Active listening shows respect. It creates trust. As we listen to our teens, we not only gain understanding, we also create an atmosphere to be understood. When parents and teens understand each others' perspectives, they can work effectively together toward solutions.

Compassion is what drives us to try to understand our teenagers. Even though we may see things differently, we seek *first* to understand. Before we speak, we listen.

Let's face it. A great deal of a teenager's behavior gives parents the opportunity to develop important character traits such as patience, understanding, and a very high tolerance for frustration. Fortunately, most of what kids do is benign. However, it helps for parents to remember that although fifteen-year-old Junior is 6 foot 4, he still is a little guy. Dr. Ross Campbell says it best:

1. Teenagers are children.
2. Teenagers will tend to act like teenagers.
3. Much of teenage behavior is unpleasant![10]

UNDER CONSTRUCTION

Our teenagers are in transition. In fact, we could almost hang a sign on their bedroom door to describe what is going on inside: "Under Construction." Our teens face pressures in their lives: physical, sexual, social, emotional, spiritual, and vocational. Here are the major changes in each area during adolescence.

1. *Physical.* Their bodies are changing, and teens must learn to accept those changes. They also must learn to use their bodies effectively. *Gangly, awkward,* and *unsure* are words sometimes associated with a teen's appearance or behavior.
2. *Sexual.* Each teen is developing a satisfying and socially accepted feminine or masculine role. He must learn how to relate to the opposite sex.
3. *Social.* Each teen must discover her own identity as a socially responsible person. She must develop and accept her own set of values and standards.
4. *Emotional.* The teen must find emotional independence from parents and other adults. Growing into an adult means learning how to be autonomous and make wise decisions.
5. *Spiritual.* The teen will begin to form his view of God independent from his parents'. He will lean to "own" his own spiritual values and have distinct spiritual experiences.
6. *Vocational.* Your teen is selecting and preparing for

an occupation. She is moving toward economic independence.[11]

These are the developmental tasks of teenagers. These are the skills and issues they need to work through to prepare for adulthood. Clearly our teenage children are "under construction," becoming independent, moving toward adulthood.

A wise parent is aware of these changes and has a strategy to help his teen work through them. Don't panic if you don't have that strategy yet! That is the purpose of this book. How might an understanding of these developmental tasks help you parent your teen? How might a lack of understanding these issues cause problems in a parent-teen relationship? Take a few minutes to think about these questions. Understanding these life stage challenges will help you make sense of your teen's thinking, feeling, and behavior. It might keep you from saying, "These are the best years of your life—enjoy them." Parenting teens effectively isn't about changing your teen; it's about understanding the changes facing your teen and helping him/her navigate them.

For "Almost Cool" Parents

1. Do you like or dislike the analogy of a teen's life being like a roller coaster ride? How accurate is the analogy?
2. Do you agree with Laurence Steinberg that "The decline of the family has been overstated"?
3. "Most parents remain the major influence on their children through adolescence and into young adulthood." Do you agree with that statement, or do you think peer pressure is stronger than a parent's influence?
4. Which of the lists were most interesting or surprising to you (and why)?
   • "Top Twelve Things Teens Want Most from Life"
   • "Teens' Views on Contemporary Issues"
   • "Feelings Teens May Experience"

5. "Under Construction" features six developmental tasks that every teenager faces. How does knowing about these tasks affect your attitude toward your teenager and parenting your teen?

Chapter 3
CHANGE YOUR PARENTING PERSPECTIVE

What is the key to successful TV parenting?" I asked a group of parents at a Chicago suburban bookstore. "What did all successful TV dads have in common? It was true of Ozzie Nelson in *Ozzie and Harriet*; it was a characteristic of Robert Young on *Father Knows Best*; and Bill Cosby always used this key parenting tool on his show. Do you know what it is?"

"They were always at home?" asked a dad.

"No, but you are close."

"They never lost their cool?" offered a mother.

"Good observation, but not what I am looking for."

"They could solve any problem in twenty-four minutes and still have time for a pudding pop?" guessed a young mother. That answer brought laughter.

"No, but that's funny. Let me put what I plan to present to you tonight into perspective. The principles from my book *The Relaxed Parent* are helpful; but if you forget all I say, if you don't buy the book, make sure you get this one key parenting aid. Do you know what I am talking about?"

Confused frowns wrinkled in unison.

"What all of these successful TV dads had was . . . a *sweater!*"

I modeled my bulky cardigan. "Even Mister Rogers subscribed to the sweater philosophy! That's the key to successful TV fathering—having the right sweater!"

The parents laughed. If only being a model father could be that easy!

I think the sweater helped those TV dads look relaxed and prepared. I don't think a white, tank top undershirt would have communicated the same level of professional, but available dad. The few guys who wore those on TV tended to yell or ignore the kids in favor of the newspaper or a TV program.

We look to those sweater-wearing dads as models. Ozzie Nelson, in his sweater and tie, would have breakfast with sons Rick and David; waited on by Harriet, wearing a freshly starched dress (with coordinating apron, also starched). Harriet would serve bacon and eggs, and Ozzie would serve timely advice that helped get the boys out of a jam. Whether it was David asking two girls to the prom, or Rick not having time to practice with his band because of his varsity sports, Ozzie always knew what to say.

I liked those old TV shows. They made me feel comforted and secure. The Nelsons could handle any dilemma. But some things were disturbing about the Nelsons, the Youngs, and the Huxtables. For one, the drudgery of an actual job never seemed to be written into the script. Sure, there might be some reference to Father working, but we rarely actually saw him work. And two, the kids seemed to be the center of these families.

The priority of the family seemed to be the children, not the marriage. Making them happy, solving their problems, coming to their rescue, seemed to be what TV parents did with most of their time. (Besides eating meals on three sides of a table. TV families never have their backs to the camera!)

CHILD-CENTERED FAMILIES

The TV families are not to blame. They are simply reflecting a common philosophy of parenting in our culture. This is the child-centered approach to parenting. What are some typical characteristics of the child-centered family?

- Asking for the child's opinion or preference on everything
- Adjusting our schedules to accommodate the child's requests
- Buying the child things he wants (but doesn't need) and not buying things we need
- Running around town chauffeuring our kids from one activity to the next, without getting time for ourselves

Today, child-centered families live on your city block and mine. I know of some children who have two or three standing obligations after school *every day.* One day, Bobby came home excited and bouncing around like a jubilant free spirit. "Come on, Billy, he told his brother. "Let's go play in the yard. Mom said today is a 'free day!' No soccer, no karate, no piano lessons! Yeah!"

That expression "free day" got to me. Bobby and Billy's mom spends hours carting her kids around town. She wants them to experience everything. It is difficult for her to say no. From her son's reaction, he might appreciate it more if she did say no.

Sometimes doing more for our kids is actually doing less.

It is so easy to place our kids on pedestals. In a way, they become idols. Our entire home life revolves around their feelings, their thoughts, their clothes, their wishes, and their activities. In a child-centered family, the parents become obsessed with their children's happiness. As author Fred Gosman warns:

43

Our obsession with our children's feeling good is simply not producing children who feel good. . . . We need to realize that effective, reasonable discipline is as much a part of love as hugs and kisses. . . . Our children . . . need to learn that . . . disappointments, sacrifices, and occasional failures are as much a part of life as party favors, soccer camps and Nintendo.[1]

PARENT-CENTERED FAMILIES

There is the other extreme, though: parent-centered families. In these homes, the parents' needs, whims, and expectations are foremost. The children are seen as servants to meet the needs of their parents. Consider David Elkind's words:

> Parents who are themselves awash in the tide of social change and are looking for self-fulfillment may have a different reaction to their teenager. A parent going through a "mid-life crisis" may be too self-absorbed with his or her own voyage of personal discovery to appreciate fully and support the needs of a teenage son or daughter.[2]

Parents are easily distracted by divorce, changes at work, the pace of social change, and stress about rearing a teenager. All the time, they may be dealing with the background emotional noise of the way it used to be, contrasted to the way it is now. The parent in a parent-centered home is so focused on his life, his needs, and his agenda, that he doesn't have the ability to consider the needs of his teenager.

Homes often become parent-centered because of stress. Financial, vocational, and marital tensions; caring for aging parents; trying to maintain their own health; and taking care of the kids pose overwhelming challenges to many parents. As a result, often "life feels like a big balancing act" and "the result is self-absorption, and the result of self-absorption is neglect of the family."[3]

In a parent-centered home, teens are seen as complements to their parents' identity. They are to mirror a positive self-image back to the parents. The teens are expected to act only in ways that reflect this positive self—"my daughter the honor roll student"; "my son the varsity football player." We want to encourage our teens to do their best, but do their best for whom? Teens can never make up for what is lacking in their parents, and they should not have to. But in parent-centered families, that is their role.

SELF-FULFILLMENT FAMILIES

The third approach to parenting is one that centers on the individual. It is not focused on the child or the parent—but every individual. Everyone pursues his or her own agenda. Each person is on a quest to be self-fulfilled. The motto of the self-fulfillment family is *What's in it for me?*

Take a look at TV, or look down the block. You don't have to peer far to discover houses that look like bus depots —people departing every few minutes for scheduled individual activities.

This is the democratic family gone to seed. Giving teenagers choices is an excellent idea, when it is appropriate. But some things are not negotiable (drugs, alcohol, and sexual activity, for instance). Teenagers need a firm hand, but not an arbitrary or unyielding one.

Recent research has demonstrated that healthy families place the family unit first and individual pursuits second. This means that the natural self-centeredness of teenagers must be challenged and modified. Raising children means helping them mature from self-centeredness to family-centeredness.

Allowing teens to pursue their own agenda, without a connection to the family, will create self-centered teens. Some parents enable this process by giving their teen lots of freedom and attention without boundaries. These parents have believed the myth that "A teen's self-esteem comes from the amount of attention she gets." Teens will soak up attention and take advantage of a lack of boundaries; but this doesn't mean that they will have positive self-esteem. Rather, it will probably mean they are self-absorbed and demanding. A critical insight for parents is that attention does not equal love or self-esteem. We want to make our teens happy, but happy in the short run may be miserable in the long run. We may create a teen who is convinced that we exist simply to please her.

According to family counselor John Rosemond, parents can give the marriage and the family priority over the whims of the teenager by doing several things:

> By making time for the marriage on a regular basis. By not catering to the child's whims, whether emotional or material. By expecting obedience, and enforcing it firmly, but gently. By presenting a united front. By acting like you know what you are doing.[4]

A BIBLICAL VIEW OF FAMILY

In contrast to the child-centered, parent-centered and self-fulfillment approaches to family, let's consider a view of family that has rarely been shown on TV—*The Waltons* in the 1970s comes the closest. This approach is based on principles from Scripture. A cultural view may be popular and comfortable, but it's focused only on the short-term. A biblical view is transcultural, takes a long-term perspective, and is inspired by our heavenly Father.

A biblical view of family finds many principles from Scripture to guide family life. Because we are looking at teenagers—a special species of children—here are five family principles that I believe are essential to rearing teenagers. And because these five elements all begin with the letter *P*, I call them *The Five P's*.

A Parent's Purpose and Priority

First, the *purpose* of people is to reflect God's image. We were created to demonstrate who God is (Genesis 1:26–27). This is an important concept for parents and teenagers to understand and embrace. God did not create us to pursue selfish interests or wrap ourselves up in making our children happy. God created us to call attention to His qualities and character. We were created to glorify God and enjoy Him forever.

Second, the *priority* of marriage is the parents. God created and blessed the husband and wife relationship before the parent-child relationship. In God's design, the marriage has *priority* over parenting. The quality of the parent-child relationship depends on the quality of the husband-wife relationship. God said "it was very good" after He created *woman*, not after He created children (Genesis 1:27–31). The marriage relationship doesn't need children to complete the family—children expand the family, they don't complete it.

Dealing with Problems

Third, the *problems* of people creates family tensions. Families are made up of people with problems. The Bible calls it sin. We have a tendency to insulate, isolate, and become independent. We like to "do our own thing." As the prophet Isaiah wrote, "We all, like sheep, have gone astray, each of us has turned to his own way; and the Lord has laid on him the iniquity of us all" (53:6).

The problem with families is that they are made up of people with problems. A biblical view of family understands that there will be problems, conflict, and disappointment. There also will need to be forgiveness, understanding, and reconciliation.

A Plan for Your Family

Fourth, God's *plan* for the family can be understood and followed. Biblical principles can be applied to raising teenagers. There is a pattern of order and a style of relating that is designed by God. In fact, the apostle Paul gives specific instructions to children and fathers in a portion of one letter.

Children, obey your parents in the Lord, for this is right. "Honor your father and mother"—which is the first commandment with a promise—"that it may go well with you and that you may enjoy long life on the earth."

Fathers, do not exasperate your children; instead, bring them up in the training and instruction of the Lord. (Ephesians 6:1–4)

Authority and order are critical for a healthy family. Children need to know that their parents are in charge. They need to obey them. This could be why this is the first commandment with a promise. Breaking God's commandment can be dangerous. I know; I saw it.

Brenda had recently received a moped for her sixteenth birthday. When her cousin Susie came over to visit, Susie wanted to try out the motor bike. But Susie's mom told her not to ride it. Susie was only fifteen, didn't know how to ride it, and was too young to ride it legally.

The warm, summer night was inviting, and Brenda decided to ride her new moped to our youth group. She asked her brother to bring Susie in his car. After the meeting, while Brenda was talking to a leader, Susie got on the moped and rode it around the parking lot. She drove faster and faster. She caught the attention of the youth in the parking lot. Some told her, "Get off Brenda's moped!"

"You don't know how to ride. *Stop!*"

But she ignored them. She sped past the group and tried to negotiate a sharp turn at the edge of the parking lot, but instead of braking, she accelerated. The wheel struck the curb, and she went airborne for twenty or thirty feet. She flew down the embankment and landed in the parking lot in the lower lot. She landed on her head.

I heard the noise and ran to her aid. She was unconscious. We immediately called 911, stabilized Susie, and prayed for her life. The paramedics came in a few minutes. For hours, she hung perilously to life, and teens from our group lined the hospital hallways, praying for her and asking questions. *What would I do if it was me?* they wondered. *Will she die?*

That was Susie's first visit to church. Susie was not from a family that attended church or believed the Bible, and her first visit to church was scary, but only because of her disobedience. Her disobedience to her mom almost cost her her life.

Obeying and honoring our parents is the first commandment with a promise: "that it may go well with you and that you may enjoy long life on the earth." God knew that for children to survive, they would need to be obedient to their parents. Susie did not know this, but if she had, she probably would not have believed it. Disobeying her mother almost killed her.

Teenagers often have problems with authority. It stands in their way to autonomy. A wise parent helps them understand that authority protects them. A parent who is able to use her authority helps protect her child and prepares her for life.

Firm yet Compassionate Parents

Fifth, God's expectations for *parents* is that they be firm yet compassionate. We need to be tough yet tender. Our teens need us to be tough when it comes to their living worthy lives but tender when they blow it. Paul was like a tender parent when he was with the Christians of Thessalonica. Thus he wrote:

> But we were gentle among you, like a mother caring for her little children. We loved you so much that we were delighted to share with you not only the gospel of God but our lives as well, because you had become so dear to us. For you know that we dealt with each of you as a father deals with his own children, encouraging, comforting and urging you to live lives worthy of God, who calls you into his kingdom and glory. (1 Thessalonians 2:7–8, 11–12)

I like to encourage parents to study this passage. It contains several qualities of an effective parent.

"Gentle": We need to be kind, and free from harshness and sternness.

"Among you": We need to be available, physically and emotionally present.

"Caring": We need to tune into our teens' needs and seek to meet them.

"Love": We need to demonstrate love by sharing and giving.

"The gospel": Christian parents seek to share the good news of Christ with their teens.

"Our lives": By connecting and being authentic, we provide models for our teens.

"Become": Parenting teens is a process. Maturity doesn't happen quickly or automatically.

"Dear to us": Our teens need an appropriate expression of our affection.

"Encouraging": Sometimes they will need us to pour courage into them.

"Comforting": At times, they will need us to comfort them; like they did when they were younger and skinned their knee. Emotionally, teens still need to "run to their parents."

"Urging": This is a strong word of discipline. It has to do with direction and motivation. Our teens need our urging to make worthwhile decisions.

"Calls us": Being a parent is a calling from God. It is a divine assignment. It is not something we take lightly. Our goal is to prepare our teens for God's kingdom and His glory.

Take a few minutes to reflect on these qualities of an effective parent. Which of these stands out as one that you would like to see developed in your own parenting?

A NEW PARENTING PERSPECTIVE

How we look at things is our *paradigm*. A *paradigm* is the way we "put things together"; it's our perspective, our order of things. Our paradigm helps us make sense of information. It helps us sort and organize. We all have a paradigm for parenting—it is our frame of reference.

We need a new frame of reference, a change in our parenting perspective. Most significant breakthroughs in technology and science required a paradigm shift, a new way of thinking. As parents, we need to leave child-centered, parent-centered, and self-fulfillment approaches and take a fresh perspective to rearing our children. With a fresh perspective, we will be able to see and understand parenting in a new and deeper way.

As Christian parents, we want to pass on lasting values to our teens. To do this, we need a perspective that is trans-cultural and not simply a product of our culture. We need a perspective that has a long-term view and is not obsessed with a short-term payoff. We need a biblical model, one based on principles that outlast the trendy voices of our current culture.

From Discipline . . .

This model uses discipline in a different way than is commonly used. As children mature, we tend to move from punishment to discipline. When our children are young we use punishment to train them. We might spank them, restrict them to their room, or from TV. Punishment is a penalty imposed on children to correct their misbehavior.

Discipline attempts to introduce the use of consequences as a means of training older children and teens. Punishment might be more appropriate for controlling and directing younger children. Logical consequences are appropriate for influencing and motivating teens. (More on consequences in chapter 4). Punishment requires a moral judgment by the parent.

"You made a mess. Go to your room!"

Consequences help the child learn moral responsibility.

"You made a mess. Clean it up."

Punishment tends to focus on the past and on behavior. Discipline tends to focus on the present and on a teen's will.

As we mature in our parenting skills, it is helpful to expand our parenting tools. We know how to use the tool of punishment. Most of us are learning to discipline using consequences. May I introduce you to a new paradigm for parenting?

. . . To Discipleship

Discipleship. Read the word carefully. I didn't say discipline. I said *discipleship*. Have you ever thought of parenting as discipleship? No, you don't have to get your teens to wear baggy, cotton tunics and sandals (though they may prefer this to what you make them wear to church!). No, you don't have to trade in the minivan for a burro and two donkeys. Discipleship isn't just for the first-century Christians walking around the Middle East. Discipleship is for modern, high-tech, suburban families (and rural, too) who have never seen a camel.

Discipleship is an intimate, personal relationship designed for growth and learning through imitation, dialogue, and observation.

The English words *disciple* and *discipline* stem from a common Latin root, *discipulus,* or "learner." Discipling is learning through an intimate, personal relationship.

Discipline should be understood not as punishment but as teaching of self-discipline, an internalization of values based on a relationship of discipleship. This kind of teaching is done by example, not by coercion or force. If we are to understand parenting as discipleship, the primary goal of parenting isn't teaching, it's modeling.

Thinking in terms of punishment focuses on behavioral control and stopping what the child is doing. Parents who think in the paradigm of discipleship, however, will focus more on what their teen is learning in relationship to them, especially in those circumstances we would consider disciplinary. Consider the words of the noted psychologist and author Bruno Bettelheim:

> The idea of discipleship implies not just the learning of specific skills and facts, but acquiring these from a master in whose image one wishes to form oneself because one admires this individual's work and life. This usually involves sustained, close personal contact, one personality being formed under the impact of the other.[5]

Parenting, like discipleship, is a teaching/mentoring relationship. Our kids are learning from us whether we intend to be teaching them or not. Teens *are* the disciples of their parents, for better or worse. Parents teach by word or example through every interaction they have with their teens.

COMPARING DISCIPLESHIP TO DISCIPLINE

Seeing parenting as discipleship helps us get a broader view of our role. Parents who only use discipline to solve an immediate problem behavior may be teaching their teens the wrong lessons. That is, "Change your behavior and I'll leave you alone." Discipleship focuses on what the teen learns, not simply changing his behavior. The chart on page 54 contrasts discipline with discipleship.

The key difference between the two approaches is that the motive of discipline is to have the child obey; the motive of discipleship is to nurture the child toward maturity. As we have noted, discipleship takes place through a personal relationship leading to growth through observation and imitation.

Study the contrasts between punishment and discipleship. How might an understanding of the differences between the two help you in your relationship with your teenager?

Chart 4	
DISCIPLINE VERSUS DISCIPLESHIP	
Discipline	**Discipleship**
Punitive	Teaching of self-discipline
Behavioral control	Growth and learning
Focus: Teen's behavior	Focus: Teen's learning
Goal: Stop misbehavior	Goal: Mentoring toward maturity
External	Internal
Personality	Character
Maintain peace in the family	Integrate personal virtues
Force	Relationship
Power	Authority
Instructional	Modeling
Reflection for the teen	Reflection for teen & parent
Battle	Tutorial
Motivation is primarily external	External & internal motivation
Compliance	Cooperation (allows for individual differences and development)
Now	A process
Action	Attitude
Submission	Mentoring
Behaving and thinking	Feeling, thinking , deciding, and behaving
Teen learns and changes	Teen *and* parent learns and changes

Have you settled for behavior change? Has discipline been more of a battle and not much learning? With discipleship, your child learns by your example rather than simply submitting to you.

I have tried to build a case for a new approach to parenting. We need to change how we perceive our role as Christian parents. Discipleship will be a new effective parenting paradigm for many of us, but it is clearly superior to the more common discipline/punishment approach, as the preceding chart shows.

Let me now attempt to describe what discipleship is *not*. Discipleship is:

- Not lecturing but living (Deuteronomy 6:5–9)
- Not only academic but caring (1 Thessalonians 2:7)
- Not sharing lessons, but sharing life (1 Thessalonians 2:8)
- Not only focused on child, but also on the parent (1 Thessalonians 2:11–12)
- Not demanding and distant, but close and empathetic (Philippians 2:5–11)

The parent who seeks to disciple his teen places himself in his teen's emotional shoes, imaginatively experiencing the world as his teen does. At the same time, he is maintaining his adult perspective, knowing that he wants to share more than lessons—he wants to share life.

For "Almost Cool" Parents

1. Besides wearing cardigan sweaters like those laid-back TV dads, what are some ways we can be more relaxed as parents?
2. Try to give an example of each family: child-centered, parent-centered, and self-fulfillment. Describe their interactions with their children.
3. Review "The Five P's" on pages 46–50. Why is each P essential for a biblical view of family?
4. Do you agree that we need a new parenting perspective? Why or why not?
5. Discuss and illustrate the contrasts between discipline and discipleship, using Chart 4.

Chapter 4
YOUR TEEN'S CHARACTER: A MATTER OF BALANCE

To develop character in our teens, we need balance. Balance is critical for many endeavors in life. Without balance, we can get ourselves in all kinds of trouble. I don't like to balance my checkbook. It's time-consuming and I'm not that good at it. But if I don't balance it, I'll be in trouble. (I thank my bank for overdraft protection!)

Balance is critical for many activities in life. For instance, I like to surf. Balance is very important for surfing; without it, you can't surf. You have to be able to balance yourself on the surfboard paddling out. You have to be able to balance sitting on the board waiting for a wave. Then balance is demanded as you paddle down the face of the wave, with gravity pulling you into the trough of the wave.

Balance is absolutely necessary when the surfer tries to stand up. You must push up and off the board as it descends down the face of the wave. You need to balance the forward pitch of the board. Too steep and you will pearl (nose-dive). Too far back on the board and you won't make the wave. You also must balance from side to side. Your weight must be evenly distributed in the middle of the board. Too much to one side will cause you to wipe out.

Then, if you have mastered all these maneuvers of balance, you're ready to surf the wave. That involves changing your position and switching your center of balance by moving your feet to different positions on the board. The constant changing of your position will help you navigate the pitching, thrusting, churning wave and allow you to stay standing.

Parenting teenagers is like surfing—you need balance. The wave of adolescence will be pitching, thrusting, and churning all around you. Your job is to maintain balance and keep standing, in spite of the turmoil around you.

Balance also helps us to develop our children's character, as well as our own. Children need a set of inner principles and a commitment to those principles as they move through adolescence toward adulthood. How do we develop such character in our children? By becoming balanced parents. Let's look at how we can develop our balance, and then we will consider how we can help our teens develop their character.

DEVELOPING YOUR BALANCE

Flexibility

Balance requires flexibility. If we are going to be able to adjust to the dramatic demands of parenting adolescents, we need to be flexible in our responses to our children and to life itself. Physically, we increase our flexibility by stretching. By stretching muscles we loosen them and increase circulation to them and the joints. Similarly, it's easy to become stiff and rigid when you are a parent of a teenager. Take some time to stretch.

Some stretching exercises for parents of teens:

- *Pull-Ups.* Give yourself a boost by treating yourself to something you enjoy. Do this guilt-free.
- *Push-Ups.* Push yourself away from the TV and talk with your teen.

- *Sit-Ups.* Sit up in your easy chair and read a helpful book (like this one!) or a magazine article which expands and stretches your understanding of teenagers.
- *Crunches.* Endure the pain of trying to find something admirable about your teenager's music or fashion.
- *Knee Bends.* Get down on your knees and pray for your teen.
- *Jumping Jacks.* Celebrate joyously with your teen when she/he has successes.

Stay in shape. The teenage years will demand your best.

Awareness

Balance also requires awareness. We need to stay alert to the ever-changing adolescent landscape around us. Balance requires our awareness of:

- Emotional issues
- Physical issues
- Spiritual issues
- Mental issues
- Relational issues

I know this is a demanding mandate. But then again, parenting adolescents is like surfing. You have to be able to balance upon a slippery surface, surrounded by an environment that is constantly changing.

Just when we get a handle on one area of our teen's life, another area might call for our attention. For instance, your teen may be acting sullen and depressed. You spend some time observing and investigating and discover it is because he is taking Spanish and hates it. There isn't anything you can do. He has to take the class. You help him survive. He pulls off a C minus. You both consider it a victory.

Then you notice he has lost weight. It seems like the stress of Spanish has caused him to lose weight. You work on that for a while only to discover that your son has had a major conflict with a friend. Do you rush in to help with that situation?

Parenting requires awareness of the various issues facing our adolescents. But it doesn't require that we are involved in all the issues of their lives. Awareness does not equal involvement. There will be some issues that we are aware of but do nothing about. Did you hear that, Super Parents? For some things *it is enough to be aware and not involved.*

Self-Control

This brings us to our third point about balance. Balance requires self-control.

There will be times when we want to rush in and rescue our teen, but it would be harmful to him if we did this. He needs to learn how to deal with some of these issues on his own. The balanced parent doesn't react to news and immediately respond to the need. He takes time to consider if this should be the issue that requires his attention and involvement. He asks himself questions like: *Does this require awareness or action? Am I the best one to respond? Is this the time to respond? If I respond to this issue, will it upset the balance with other issues in my teen's life?*

Balance requires self-control. It will help us to not overreact to our teens. Self-control will also help us not react to our teens when they push our buttons.

You know what I mean. Our buttons are our places of emotional vulnerability. These are points of great emotion and sometimes frustration. Our teens have studied these for years. They know which ones to push and when. They have studied our buttons, sometimes more than math. There is reinforcement for a child who knows how to choose and use her parent's buttons. It's fun for a teen to make her parent respond to her maneuverings.

When we don't respond to our teen's button pushing, it takes away the fun for the teen. It reduces the payoff of controlling the parent. To work toward this, let me ask you, *What are your hot buttons?*

Take a few minutes and list behaviors that your teen does to make you react. If you don't mind marking a book, fill in the buttons below.

My hot buttons: ❒ _____

❒ _____

❒ _____

When our kids push our buttons, causing us to react, we have lost our self-control. We lose our balance. They have us off-balance. In a way, they have taken control. What can we do to maintain our self-control?

Remember that parenting is dynamic, not static. It is in a continual state of flux. Parenting isn't an exact science. It's more of an art. When we have proven principles that have been forged through experience, we have the tools to shape our art form.

There are no guarantees in parenting. No fool-proof formulas. Our teens have a way of tampering with formulas anyway. What worked for the first kid won't work for the second. All the more reason why we need to stay current and flexible with our parenting. When I say flexible, I don't mean compromising and wimpy. I mean anticipating the challenges and changes and being prepared for them. The key strategy, as youth speaker Ken Davis says, is balance:

> The key word is *balance*. Every action a parent takes is most effective when it is balanced with another action. And that's not easy—it requires thought, consideration for the feelings of your child, and a tremendous amount of self-control. Fortunately, the rewards for all that effort go beyond positively influencing your child's growth. It is also rewarding to see your own continued growth as a parent as you begin to experience some measure of control—both of yourself and of your relationship with your son or daughter.[1]

CHARACTER RAISING

In my mind, parents are either raising characters or building character. What does it mean to build our teen's character? It means to prepare her for life, from the inside out. It's more than teaching rules. It's more than passing on family values. It's about developing our teen's inner commitment to principle. Motivate your teen inwardly—shape her character—and you will motivate her to good and noble outward behavior.

Balanced parents know that it's important to help our children grow internally as well as externally. We want to give them nourishment and exercise for a healthy body. We want to give them God's Word and spiritual disciplines for a healthy soul.

When we have balance, our watching children see a model for character and consistency. As family expert Wes Haystead notes, "The parent will see in the child a reflection of what the child has seen in the parent."[2]

This is the biblical principle of modeling. If we want to see a quality produced in the lives of our teens, we need to live it out in front of them. This is part of our role as disciplers of our teens. When it comes to character, more is caught than taught.

We can give our teens many things to help launch them towards success in life, but one of the most lasting and helpful is a foundation of character. An important twenty-year study by Harvard professor Robert Coles, author of *The Spiritual Life of Children*, concluded that "parents who want to give their children the best chance for success in life will teach them strong moral values."[3]

Character prepares our teens for life because it gives them integrity of soul. They don't have to pretend. They don't have to act. They are the same on the outside as on the inside. No surprises. A teenager with character is consistent, inside and out.

Some teenagers are more determined. We often call them

"strong-willed." We build the character of a strong-willed adolescent not by destroying his will, but rather by redirecting it.

CHARACTER AND BALANCE

I believe that a person with character is balanced. She knows what is important. She doesn't chase after things that are temporary or have no lasting value.

The Bible teaches that balance is a key part of Christlike character. As the apostle Paul wrote, "For God did not give us a spirit of timidity, but a spirit of power, of love and of self-discipline" (2 Timothy 1:7). Notice the balance. There is a built-in balance, with power on one end and love on the other. In the middle, there is self-discipline. Picture it like a teeter-totter:

On one end of the teeter-totter we see that God has provided us with a spirit of power. Power to take on the challenges of parenting teenagers. Strength to hang in there when we feel like quitting. This is the power of God's Spirit within us. God has not given us a wimpy, timid, this-is-too-big-for-me attitude. If you have that attitude, it's not from God.

On the other end of the teeter-totter, we see *love*. God has given us a spirit of love. Love to take on the challenges of parenting teenagers. Love to give them when they are most unlovable. That is when they need it the most. That calls for unconditional love. Such love is unnatural. In fact, it is supernatural. That kind of love comes from the Spirit of God.

Notice the beautiful balance. At times, parenting teens demands power we don't have. God promises power. There will be times when we just don't have the love to give our teens. God promises love. Power and love. Love and power. Which do you need?

Chances are, if you have teens, you need both. You will need the ability to go from one to another. That is what makes this verse so meaningful to me. Notice what else God offers us: self-discipline. Self-discipline is the balance and the ability to go from power to love and back as we need it. A self-disciplined person is a balanced person. An undisciplined person is someone who has lost his balance. He is doing too much of something. A drunk has lost his balance because he drinks too much. An obese person has lost balance of his diet. A frantic, stressed worker has lost his or her balance because of too many things to do in too little time.

Balance and self-discipline are two qualities we want to see in our teens. If they see those qualities in us, we are more apt to see those qualities in our teens. Teens believe what they *see* in you over what they hear you *say*.

USING CONSEQUENCES

We can help our teens develop character and prepare them for life by using consequences. In a way, it is a life simulation.

When our children were smaller we would discipline them if they broke the rules. If they stole cookies; no dessert. If they didn't take a nap, they would go to bed early. Discipline that was clear and concrete, black and white.

It's not that easy with teens. Discipline becomes gray. Teens challenge our discipline. They spend huge amounts of mental energy to avoid or manipulate our discipline endeavors. This requires a shift in strategy. As youth pastor Daniel Hahn writes:

> Parents face two options. We can keep using the same patterns we used when they were young (and frustrate ourselves to death), or we can realize that our methods must change as our kids develop. . . . As hard as it is, our role must move from controller to consultant. What do consultants do? They ask questions, offer opinions, share experiences, present options and forecast outcomes. Ultimately, however, they

step back and allow the client to make decisions. Consultants understand what they can and cannot do for their client, and as a result the client owns the process as well as the results. The fact is, as kids grow up we can't control much of what they do anyhow. . . . Our best shot is influence.[4]

A consultant uses consequences, not just rules. A rules-only approach puts too much responsibility on the shoulders of the parent. By using consequences, a parent can teach teens to assume responsibility for their own behavior.

Using consequences for your teens' behavior will hold them accountable. Let them know in advance what those consequences will be. Include your teens in developing specific consequences for their specific behavior. But do this in advance of needing it. Don't wait until you have a problem to think up a consequence. Anticipate which consequences you will need and discuss these with your teenagers.

For instance, what should you do if your teenage daughter continually forgets to pick up her dirty clothes? You have several options. As a parent, you can: (1) leave them there and ask her to pick them up; (2) throw them under your teen's bed; (3) throw them in the trash; (4) restrict her to her room until she cleans it up; or (5) another option of your choice.

We discussed this situation with a group of parents of teenagers. One single mother, Debra, had fallen into the habit of nagging her daughter to pick up her clothes, books, and assorted "junk." Debra reported her solution: a cardboard box with "Saturday" written on the side of it.

"I told my daughter that if she left her stuff out, it would go in the 'Saturday Box,' and she could get it out on Saturday." The one exception was schoolbooks. "Everything else she would just have to live without."

With those clear consequences, her daughter quickly complied.

"You should see our house," Debra told us. "None of her stuff is trashing it like it used to."

Your own strategies for dirty rooms, curfews, and other issues will vary. The important thing is to choose those consequences, inform your children, and then stick to them.

TWO KINDS OF CONSEQUENCES

Natural Consequences

Consequences fall into two categories: natural and logical. Natural consequences are the results of choices we make that are subject to the laws of nature. Throw a rock into the ocean, it will sink. Jump out of an airplane, you will sink. Forget the parachute, and you will die. All those are natural consequences. At your funeral, they can say, "He died of natural causes—gravity."

Our teens can learn from natural consequences. But some are too severe to be good teachers. We don't say, "If you drink and drive you may get in a wreck." Instead we command them: "Don't drink, and certainly not when you are going to drive." We want to protect our teens from the full impact of natural consequences.

In addition, some natural consequences are not immediate enough for the teen to learn from them. This is why we need logical consequences. Logical consequences are outcomes decided on by the parent, usually with the teen's input, that discipline wrong behavior. To be effective, logical consequences must seem logical to the teenager. They must make sense and seem appropriate. Logical consequences need to be reasonably connected to the misbehavior.

Logical Consequences

Unlike natural consequences, which often take years to occur, logical consequences are typically immediate. Daniel Hahn, author of *Teaching Your Kids the Truth About Consequences*, emphasizes the impact of logical consequences:

These are situations we *design* in order to teach an immediate lesson, to prove the logic of a certain course of action or direct behavior. Logical consequences, when used appropriately, speak volumes and have a far greater impact than any parental lecture ever could. Capitalizing on the influential power of felt results in daily situations helps children see just how real consequences actually are. And here's the real punch: *kids learn to respect the reality of long-term, natural consequences when parents use short-run, logical consequences as a routine part of shaping behavior.* [5]

We used logical consequences recently. It was time to purchase back-to-school clothes. With two teenage daughters, this is no small feat. Ed McMahon had not stopped by with a check for a million dollars, so I knew things would be tight. My wife, Suzanne, and I discussed the situation. We figured how much money we could afford to spend on clothes. In previous years, we had set the budget and overspent it, using credit cards, promissory notes, second mortgage on the house, and loan sharks.

This year we were determined to stick to the budget. And this year's budget was smaller than last year's. It was going to be a challenge. Prices had gone up and so had their tastes.

We offered them cash.

"Here is the money for your back-to-school clothes. This is all we have. Notice this green stuff is cash. We aren't using plastic. I know that comes as a shock to you, but we want to prepare you for life. A life without those easy credit plans. You can go to the mall and get a few things. You will have a bag you can be proud of, but you won't have a lot of clothes. Or, you can shop the discount stores and outlets and you'll have more. It's your choice. It's your money."

Nicole and Brooke took the money, counted it, and immediately tore into the print ads from the newspaper.

"Dad, will you take me to the mall? They are having a sale at the department store."

"Sure, Brooke. Is that how you want to spend you clothing allowance?"

"Yeah, Dad, these tops are sooo cool!"

Fifteen minutes later, we were looking at the cool tops in the hip, young women's section in the department store.

"Dad, here they are! Doesn't this look cool?"

"Yeah, it does. It's very cool. How much is it?"

"It's thirty-eight dollars." As she read the price tag, I could see her mental gears working.

"Are you going to get it?"

"If I get that, I won't have much money to get anything else. I need more than one top."

"What do you want to do, Brooke?"

"Can we go to the discount store?"

"You mean the one twenty minutes away?"

"Yeah, they are having tops like this on sale for ten dollars each."

"You mean, you could get three for the price of one?"

"Yeah. And I would still have money left over for shoes."

Brooke loves shoes.

We made the journey to the big discount store. We discovered some cool tops.

"Dad! Can you believe it? These are better than the ones at the department store, and they are marked down. They are only eight dollars! I am going to get four!"

Our girls learned how to stretch a dollar this fall. They wound up doing very well with the limited amount we gave them. Best of all, they took pride in their discoveries. They looked good, too. I think they wore their clothes with confidence because they worked at putting together their wardrobe. It didn't come easy. And it didn't come on plastic.

DEVELOPING LOGICAL CONSEQUENCES

To help you develop logical consequences for your teenager, follow these five steps:

1. *Define your expectations.* Your teen needs to know what you expect. Don't assume that she knows.
2. *Develop logical consequences for a few select areas.* Discuss these in advance with your teenager. "Before you go to your friend's, I want you to know that I expect you to spend the entire night there. Not be out anywhere else. If you do, you will lose the privilege of staying at his house for awhile. Agreed?"
3. *Develop with your teenager logical consequences.* Involve them in the process, especially for the bigger issues: dating, driving, drinking and drugs. Helping teens develop their own consequences will remind them that they are responsible for their own behavior.
4. *Put it in writing.* Put your agreed-upon consequences into a formal document. Recording the list of consequences will remind your teen of what she agreed to and assures you that both she and you live up to the agreement. Have a place for your teen's and your signatures. Make sure you keep a copy for yourself. These things have a tendency to disappear for some reason.
5. *Refer to and enforce the document.* Refer to the written document of logical consequences when necessary. Enforce the consequences. Remind your teen that these consequences are a result of choices they made. Consequences that they helped determine.[6]

Those five steps are key, yet there is one more thing we should do to apply logical consequences. Actually, it's not an action but an attitude. *Relax and watch consequences work.*

There's no need for shouting, threatening, or stressing about discipline. It has already been determined. Your job, as parent, is to *be consistent and firm with the application* of the consequence. For example:

"I see you chose to come in a half hour past the agreed upon time. What is the consequence?"

"I dunno."

"Go get the paper."

"I lost it."

"Oh, would you look at that! I happen to have a copy here. What does it say?"

"It says I have to come in early next time, twice as many minutes as I was over this time."

"How much is that?"

"I was only a half hour over!"

"Then that would be sixty minutes, wouldn't it?"

"Yeah."

"OK. Next time you want to go out, you will come in sixty minutes earlier than usual. Got it?"

"Yeah."

"Now, hand me the remote control, please; I'm going to watch 'Wild Kingdom.'"

Reduce the anxiety of raising your teen by being prepared to discipline him with effectiveness. Understand that character will impact the choices your teen makes. This really follows the biblical principle that "a man reaps what he sows. The one who sows to please his sinful nature, from that nature will reap destruction" (Galatians 6:7–8). Help him make wise choices by learning from consequences. Logical consequences can help your teen avoid destructive actions and make wise choices, choices that will grow his character.

For "Almost Cool" Parents

1. Which of the stretching exercises for parents of teens (see "Flexibility") do you think you need the most?
2. Balance as parents includes being flexible (interacting and being sensitive to our teens), being aware of issues in our teens' lives, and having self-control. Why is balance essential in these areas?
3. Why is providing a positive example so important in helping develop our teens' character?

4. What are some of the advantages of using consequences instead of rules to discipline a teenager?
5. Explain the difference between natural and logical consequences. Why should we seek logical consequences instead of letting natural consequences run their course?

Chapter 5
TALKING WITH YOUR TEEN

What is it about parenting that makes us say silly things? Chances are you were much more articulate before you had kids. You were able to converse with friends on a plethora of subjects. Your vocabulary was larger. You actually used words like *plethora* and knew what they meant.

Parents have one thing in common—our kids prompt us to make stupid comments.

For instance, the other night Nicole brought over a young man who was going to take her to homecoming at their high school. We, as caring parents, wanted to meet this guy.

"So, you are going to homecoming with my daughter?"

"Yes, sir."

Nicole grimaced.

"Do you know what you will be driving?"

"Yes, my father's car."

"What kind of car is it?" I inquired.

"It's an Oldsmobile."

"Fine, fine. Is anyone else going with you?"

"Yes. Jason and Courtney."

"I see . . . The four of you together; in one car. Are you going to dinner?"

"Yes. We were thinking of the steak place."

"Fine choice. They have nice booths there."

The young man shifted uncomfortably in his chair.

Nicole was rolling her eyes and turning pale.

"So you play baseball, do you?"

"Yes, sir."

"Do you have a pretty good team this year?"

"Yeah, I mean yes; we look pretty strong."

"You're on varsity?"

"Yes."

"What position?"

"Pitcher."

"Great. Well thanks for coming over. We wanted to meet you before you take Nicole to homecoming. By the way, what's your curfew?"

"My folks say I have to be in by 1:00 A.M."

"Sounds reasonable for homecoming. Thanks for stopping by. We wanted to meet you and let you know what is important to us before you take our daughter out. I know it seems a little old-fashioned, but she is our baby, you know."

Nicole drops her jaw in embarrassment, *"Daad!"* She turned crimson.

"Ummm . . . yes sir."

See what I mean? Being a parent of a teenager makes us say silly stuff. Nicole told me later that the whole conversation was painful enough, but the killer was when I said, "she is our *baby*, you know." This just about made her crawl under the sofa cushion.

She asked me, "Why did you say that, Dad?"

"I'm not sure. I wanted him to sense that you are important to us. I wanted him to understand how we see you."

"As a baby? You see me as a baby?"

"No. But I see you as a sixteen year old who *used* to be our baby."

She frowned, shook her head, and walked out.

Why do we say these things? We can be normal, in-control adults, who can usually pull off a decent conversation; but get us around teenagers and we say the dumbest things.

Recently, I was talking with a group of parents about how our teens bring out the stupid comments in us. One of the moms told the story of her son preparing for homecoming.

"I had Mark bring his date to our house before they left. I wanted to take pictures. I provided some snacks and soda for them and three other couples. I lined them all up for a group shot. They looked so handsome and beautiful. The girls were so gorgeous it scared me. Then it happened. Right after I took the picture, they darted to get in the car; as they were getting in, I warned, 'Just say no!' Can you believe it? Why did I say that?"

"What did Mark do?" I asked.

"He gave me The Look."

Sometimes the tension of parenting teens causes us to say the silliest things. But it's not entirely our fault. We learned it from our parents. Can you remember some of the inane things your parents said? You probably drove them to say it. Perhaps now you hear yourself saying the same things.

"I'm doing this for your own good."

"I have been worried sick. Where have you been?"

"You are grounded for the rest of your life!"

"Don't look at me with that tone of voice!"

HOW TO TALK "GOODER"

It is often difficult to communicate with teenagers. Sometimes just trying leads to more conflict. It's a recurring dilemma, according to psychologist Haim Ginott: "Parents of teenagers face a difficult dilemma: how to help when help is resented, how to guide when guidance is rejected, how to communicate when attention is taken as attack."[1]

A Parent's Fantasy

As adults, we really value communication: the giving and receiving of messages. We may even fantasize about communicating with our teens. At a recent parents' seminar, I asked, "What is your parenting fantasy?"

A mother raised her hand to respond, "My fantasy is coming home from work. The laundry is done; the house is picked up. Our teens have finished their homework and have prepared a tasty and well-balanced meal. We sit at the table and leisurely talk in the candlelight. No phones. No rush. Just time to connect."

Does this sound real to you? I didn't think so. This is not very common. As a result, many parents feel a sense of failure, *Something must be wrong with me.*

We feel guilty when we can't live up to the communication fantasy. But don't worry. You can dismiss your dream of effective communication with your teenager. It's unrealistic and unnecessary. Effective communication is learned by adults and practiced by adults. Don't expect teens to communicate like you. They don't need to "communicate" like adults. They talk and listen in a way uniquely their own.

In fact, teens feel outgunned by their parents' communication skills. In the teens' eyes, parents bring a heavy cannon to the conversation, with larger vocabulary, fancier sentences, more poise, and much experience. Most teens don't feel equipped to duel their parents with conversation.

You may not sense that your relationship with your teen is adversarial, but in a way it is. You have something they want, and you are not sure you want to give it to them. You know what it is? Freedom. Autonomy. Being on their own. But they are not there, yet. That is why you let out the leash slowly. You give them more freedom as they demonstrate they can handle it.

The same is true of communication. It is developmental. It takes time to acquire the skills of communication. Most teens aren't very confident talking with adults. Communicating with teens is different from communicating with adults.

A Whole Different Approach to Talking

The difference between adult and teen communication is significant—the whole approach is different. Adults like to communicate with reason and logic. In contrast, teens tend to be more stream of conscious.

As adults, we communicate in a straight line. We say: "A equals B, and B equals C, so A equals C." That's logical and linear, and that's how we prefer to communicate. Adults prefer to stick to one topic at a time. We usually stay at one level of conversation. Not too personal; not too self-revealing. We value listening and try not to interrupt each other. We usually let each other finish our thoughts. We don't always say whatever runs through our mind.

With teens, though, if a new thought is on their mind, it is on their lips. They don't mind switching topics, just like they don't mind channel surfing the TV. Teens don't mind interrupting each other or changing the subject. They don't like to stay on one topic too long.

For example, consider this campus conversation:

"Michelle, I saw John today. He talked to me at lunch."

"Cool. How did he look?"

"Normal. Nothing really hip."

"Hey, speaking of hip, did you see the new lime green display at 'Charlottes' in the mall? The clothes look so cool!"

"What's there?"

"Short skirts, bells, crop tops, knits—you name it."

"I saw Brandon in the mall. He was with Aaron. He's such a loser."

"I heard Aaron got busted in biology."

"Mr. Benson is such a jerk. He kicked him out for such a small deal. It was just a little fire."

"I'm choking in biology. My parents are grounding me. I can't go to the game this weekend."

"Oh no! Who will I go with? I don't want to go with Patty, she'll probably do something obnoxious."

"I wonder if Darren and Sean will be there?"

"You know Sean is 'available' now?"

"Of course. I can't believe Kendra dumped him. She's dumb. She's got the worst taste in music"

"Hey look, here comes Sean now. He looks fine today."

Could you follow along? Don't worry if you could not. The speakers hopped from topic to topic, never stopping long enough to develop one idea. Such a conversation may seem pointless and random. But it's part of how teenagers speak. In fact, teens speak a different language; we need interpreters.

Teenagers talk because they enjoy the company. They don't have to have a point. They don't have to "get to the bottom-line." They don't have to fix anything or come to any conclusions. Most of their world is open-ended anyway.

Adults have a totally different view of communication. They use it to solve problems, to move product, and to change behavior. They are solution-oriented. Teens tend to be more process-oriented. They are often content to talk with each other for hours without anyone offering any solutions.

The secret to communicating with teens is to relax. We need to focus on how to talk and listen, not deep communication. We also need to speak their language. Your teenager is from another culture. If you don't believe me, just look at her room! Foreign cultures frequently are known to have a foreign language. If you want to communicate to a foreigner, you need to learn her language.

OBSTACLES TO COMMUNICATION

Forgetting What It's Like Being a Teen

One of the barriers to conversations with your teen *is forgetting what it is like to be a teen*. Sometimes it is easier to stay in our adult culture and not take the risk of going into the strange and alien adolescent world.

H. Stephen Glenn and Jane Nelsen, in their book *Raising Self-Reliant Children in a Self-Indulgent World,* call this obstacle an "adultism."

> An *adultism* occurs any time an adult forgets what it is like to be a child and then expects, demands, and requires of the child, who has never been an adult, to think, act, understand, see and do things as an adult. These unrealistic expectations from adults produce impotence, frustration, hostility and aggression in young people. . . . The language of adultisms is, "Why can't you ever? How come you never? Surely you realize! How many times do I have to tell you? Why are you so childish? When will you ever grow up? Did you? Can you? Will you? Won't you? Are you? Aren't you?"[2]

Trying to Understand Too Much or Seeking Closure

The wise parent understands that a good way to shut down conversations with her teen is to *try to understand too much.* Sometimes parents try to know all the details and have a complete comprehension of the facts. This can drive teens crazy, or at least, drive them away. When we try to understand too much, teens may feel like they are being interrogated.

Author William Coleman suggests several practical ways to create a relaxed, friendly setting that invites conversation without seeking specific answers or a full discourse:

> Everyone is more likely to open up at a ball game, on a shopping trip, or out to dinner. One of our family's favorite outings was to go to the coffee shop. Relaxing, munching on bread sticks, and sipping a soft drink helped our teenagers and ourselves to open up. No agenda. We weren't fishing for inside information. Just shooting the breeze, letting the conversation flow. It helped us learn a great deal about one another as we explored subjects we never anticipated discussing.[3]

Another obstacle is *always seeking closure*. Teens are happy to leave things open-ended. There doesn't always have to be "a point." There doesn't have to be a moral or a lesson. There doesn't have to be a conclusion, a summary, or an application. Those tend to be parent things, not teen things.

ON THE ROAD TO GOOD CONVERSATIONS

Teens will talk if they feel comfortable and safe. Just as Coleman points out the value of a coffee shop to open up conversation, other settings outside the home can help get teens to talk. Many parents have discovered that a good place to talk with their teen or preteen is in the car.

"I had to take a six-hour trip to San Francisco. I invited my daughter to go with me. It was just the two of us. I look forward to trips like this," a mother of two teens told me. "As you know, there isn't a lot to see, so we talked. I tried to do more listening than talking, and my fifteen-year-old daughter really jabbered. She talked almost the whole trip."

A road trip, alone with our teens, can be the best place to talk. No interruptions. No phones. No pesky younger siblings.

Most teens feel comfortable in a vehicle. They don't feel so outgunned with you sitting in the Chevy. Most teens actually feel empowered here. In a car, teens feel prepared to change the subject. The road provides creative interruptions. Teens like built-in distractions. Road trips offer built-in distractions. When teens feel things are fair, they are open to dialogue.

As drivers, parents are forced to keep their eyes on the road. This makes it feel safer to the teen. He's thinking, *I guess it is OK to talk. At least they aren't staring at me with their stupid eye contact. If it gets too intense, I'll create a dialogue diversion.*

When a parent and a teen are driving in a car the wise teen knows he is safer than being in the living room. At home, the parent can seize any opportunity for a "teachable moment."

For example, the cat gets spooked by the neighbor's

Weed Whacker and darts through the house, knocking over the dog's water dish. The dog gets mad and chases the cat up the new curtains.

The parent seizes the opportunity.

"You see, son, fear caused the new curtains to become Shredded Wheat."

"What, Dad?"

"Fear, my son. *Fear!* It can make us react in harmful ways. Did you notice how Fluffy ran because of fear? Many times we are tempted to run because of fear. Fear can make us do things that we regret."

"*What*, Dad?"

"Son, the only thing to fear is fear itself. Why I think you should . . . blah-blah-blah-blah-blah . . ."

Teens feel vulnerable at home. At any moment they could fall prey to the *teachable moment.*

But in a car, they have some power, as Dad must keep his eyes on the road (at least we hope so). If he tries to offer a teachable moment, the teenage son can easily point at something. For instance:

"Hey, Dad. Did you see that red sports car? Big guy in there. It looked like Michael Jordan! Speed up and let's take a look."

Not wanting to be a stale father-figure, Dad presses the accelerator and catches up with the Corvette, only to discover it's some guy in his sixties.

The teen feels victorious because he strategized his way out of a teachable moment.

TIPS ON TEEN TALK

Here are four tips for talking with your teen. Practice these suggestions and you may have enjoyable, even meaningful, conversations with your maturing child.

1. Be Alert to Your Teen's Limitations.

Parent-teen communication is limited to the understanding of the teenager. You may not like this, but there is little you can do to change it. Our teens have limitations.

We cannot make our teens into mini-adults. They have limitations because they are adolescents. They have limitations with time and focus. They can't talk about a topic for lengthy periods, and they are easily distracted by another topic. They also have limitations with experience and with relationships. Their experiences that help them interpret reality are minimal, and their human resources are much less than those of their parents.

Thus teens enter a conversation with an adult with serious limitations. The wise parent understands the limits of teenage communication and adjusts his strategy. Even with these limitations, though, teenagers are more apt to join us for dialogue as long as they sense we care and will listen to their side. I like the way H. Stephen Glenn and Jane Nelsen discuss dialogue:

> A dialogue is a meaningful exchange of perceptions in a non-threatening climate of support and genuine interest. Without engaging in genuine dialogue with people of importance to them, our young people find it difficult to perceive themselves as meaningful and significant. And yet, dialogue is surfacing in research as the foundation of critical thinking, moral and ethical development, judgmental maturity, bonding, closeness, and trust. . . .
>
> Three perceptions are necessary before closeness and trust can be established in a relationship:
>
> 1. This person is listening to me.
> 2. I can risk my perceptions and feelings here without being discounted for them.
> 3. This person's behavior toward me indicates that what I think or have to offer is significant.[4]

2. Remember the 50 Percent Rule.

Talk 50 percent of the time or less. That is the 50 percent

rule. You are 50 percent responsible for conversations with your teen; try to make your teen pick up the other 50 percent. In fact, when possible, spend more time listening than talking.

I often meet parents who say, "I can't get my teen to talk with me! There must be something wrong with her. I fix a nice dinner, we eat it together, I ask her 'How was school?' and all she gives me is, 'Fine.' What is her problem?"

I introduce the parent to the 50 Percent Rule.

"If you want to talk with your teen, realize that you are at least 50 percent responsible. Don't blame her for not talking with you. You have the authority and the experience that will give you a strategy for talking with your teen. It's not all your fault and it's not all hers. Assume 50 percent of the responsibility, and see what happens."

In prodding your teen to speak her 50 percent, try to find a place where your teen feels comfortable. Create an atmosphere where teens will talk.

> Teenagers prefer informal settings for engaging in conversation with their parents. They don't like family conferences or twenty questions at the dinner table. A casual atmosphere, like the kitchen or family room, is more natural and more comfortable for everyone. Standing around in the kitchen during meal preparation, for instance, got high marks by both males and females [teenagers]. It's a setting in which they don't feel trapped or on the spot. They can either change the topic or leave if they need to.[5]

If your teen feels comfortable, she is more apt to open up and talk with her mom or dad.

Use your experience and authority to develop a strategy. I think this tip can help us parents relax. We know we aren't 100 percent at fault for weak communication. It relieves some guilt. We can back off a little, knowing we need only give it our best shot; it still may not work. In other words, we shouldn't expect our wishes to automatically become our teens'. Some parents assume that because they want to communicate with their teen, the teen should want to communicate with them. But wishing is not an effective parenting tool.

3. Avoid the Conversation Killers

Teens get defensive when we speak for them. When talking with your teenager, try to lead your sentences with phrases like, "I feel" or "I think." These are more likely to lead to dialogue than phrases like, "You are (a spoiled brat)" or "You always (talk back)", or even, "You never (do your chores)."

These are three conversation killers:
"You are . . ."
"You always . . ."
"You never . . ."

On this issue, what works with us will generally work with our teens. Talking with authorities can be a tense situation. Your teen talking to you is like you talking with your boss.

What would happen at work, if your boss cornered you and exclaimed, "*You are* late with that project!"?
"It's because . . ."
"*You always* are so creative at making excuses."
"What do you mean? I was just . . ."
"*You never* clean up your workstation before leaving!"
Uncomfortable, isn't it?

Treat your teens like you would like to be treated. It's the Golden Rule applied to parenting: "Do unto your teens as you would have others do unto you."

That is why it is helpful to speak for yourself, not for others. That's a real conversation killer. When you are seeking to have dialogue with your teen, don't speak for her. If you do, then she may feel she doesn't have anything to say.

It helps to be a little tentative with teenagers. Instead of saying, "This is what I think . . .", which the teen interprets *I have to agree with Dad or I lose my freedom,* Try being a little more tentative:

"I think it could be a choice between option A and option B. Which do you think is better? Why?"

Help your teen learn to exercise discernment. Help him develop the ability to think and make wise decisions. Provide time for him to consider the options and discuss them with you.

When your teen believes you want his input, and are willing to listen to his perspective, then he is much more likely to converse with you.

4. Spend Time with Your Teen

Teens communicate that they like their friends by spending time with them. It is their language of love. I am always leery about the parent who says: "We don't have a lot of time, but the five minutes we have each day is *quality time.*"

This may be the way the parent thinks, but a teen has a different perspective. Teens are more process-oriented. They aren't as eager as adults to get to the bottom line, to complete the task.

Have you noticed that teens are on their own timetable? You can't rush them. They like to do some things very slowly. Like get dressed when you are in a hurry and needed to leave twenty minutes ago!

"Quality time" is a myth created by adults. It imagines that teens can act like adults. *If we treat them like adults, they will act and talk like adults,* goes the reasoning. The concept of quality time is driven by the need of the parents, who often are overcommitted and try to assign a few minutes of their hectic schedules to activities devoted to their children and call it "quality time."

But teenagers demand a lot of time and effort. Our patience and presence show our concern, a critical virtue when it comes to parenting teens. William Coleman compares good conversation to cultivating our garden, especially with teens:

Conversation takes time to cultivate, like a garden. Parents are generally in a hurry. Consequently, they tend to want short, concise conversations, but expect them at the same time to be deep revealing and personal—almost an impossible combination.

Statistics show that most fathers spend only three minutes a day talking to their children. Almost all the teenagers I spoke to said this is fairly accurate. Instant rapport with anyone, no less our teenagers, is a pipe dream. We are looking for something like a microwave conversation. We want to punch up three minutes on the timer and start sharing with each other, expecting instant understanding and camaraderie.[6]

There are no shortcuts to a harvest. We need to put in the time, cultivating, watering, and waiting if we want to see the bounty. We won't always be able to see the fruit of our labor. But if we skip the work in the garden, we will miss the harvest—the fruit of enjoyable dialogue with our son or daughter.

Parenting can be so messy. It doesn't fit into the constraints of our Day-Timers. Our teen could actually demand more time than what we have allotted in our schedules. They often do.

The almost cool parent has discovered that he needs to regularly schedule blocks of time with his teen. As a result, he has time to actually relax with his teen, increasing the potential for meaningful dialogue.

At Christmas, we attempted to assemble one of those "easy to assemble" foosball tables. Starting at 4:00 P.M., Nicole, Brooke, and I were anxious to put it together and start playing. *Five hours later* we played our first game. We had hours to talk, get frustrated, assemble, reassemble, laugh, talk, snack, get mad at the goofy instructions, talk, and *finally* play. It may not be your idea of quality time, but just the amount of time allowed us some great conversations. Like, "Dad, I'm glad you are a writer and not a mechanic!"

For "Almost Cool" Parents

1. Why do you think being a parent of a teenager makes us say stupid stuff?
2. Some parents expect honest, regular communication with their teenagers. Others throw up their hands and say, "What's the use? I give up." What are your expectations for communicating with your teen?
3. Which of the obstacles to communication with your teen seem to be familiar to you: (1) forgetting what it's like to be a teen, (2) trying to understand too much, (3) always seeking closure, or (4) trying to make every moment a teachable moment?
4. Discuss the four "Tips on Teen Talk." With which one are you effective? Which one would you like to improve on?
5. Are teens like gardens? What do you think about the comparison?

Chapter 6
HANDLING THE HORMONE HURRICANE

Puberty can be a very confusing time for a teenager. The changes just in his or her body can be very perplexing; there also are major emotional and social changes. Along with the confusion, go many myths which only add to the bewilderment. I asked a group of parents to share some of the myths that they used to believe when they were teens. Here are their *Puberty Follies*:

- Boys with large Adam's apples are sexually mature.
- Girls with large breasts are more interested in sex.
- Girls can only get pregnant during their period.
- Venereal disease germs can be washed away in the shower.
- A bad case of acne indicates a variety of sexual problems.
- People can tell if you have had sex by how you walk.

Can you identify with any of these? If you think about these for a while, they take you back to a bewildering and exciting period called puberty. But we don't have to panic—we have been there. We are puberty survivors!

In this chapter we will learn how to handle the hormone hurricane. We can reduce the anxiety and panic of puberty if we are willing to understand the issues of puberty and respectfully discuss these with our teenager.

Panic is certainly one of the emotions we encounter when our child hits puberty. Barry St. Clair and his wife, Carol, youth ministry veterans and founders of Reach Out Ministries, understand:

> Panic! That one word best describes the response of parents when children "hit" adolescence. It sure describes ours. We have worked with young people for more than twenty years and have spoken to thousands of young people around the world. We have held many seminars for parents on how to raise their children. That made us "experts" in working with young people. (Notice the past tense.)
>
> Now we have teenagers on our own. It's a whole new ball game. In fact, we think we have switched leagues—maybe even changed sports. When Scott crashed into adolescence, we crashed with him. As much as we thought we were prepared, we were not.
>
> Panic! It came from every direction. What made us fearful?
>
> • His body grew eight inches in twelve months. One month he was a skinny little tyke with braces and glasses; the next he had grown into a man.
> • Barry's closet emptied because Scott now wore the same size clothes.
> • Zits appeared. He started ordering Seabreeze by the gallon. [Today teens would order Clearasil.]
> • The food bill skyrocketed. His appetite alone [raised] the food bill almost $100.00 a month.
> • Emotions rode a roller coaster. One day he was as high as a kite, the next day he was in "Pit City."

- Responsibility grew—and wavered. One day he acted like an adult. The next day he acted like a first-grader.
- Hormones became active. His once-baby-smooth face needed a shave.
- Women were discovered. Girls no longer had cooties; instead they received mega-attention.
- And in no time, he will be gone.[1]

Puberty means changes and lots of them, including a teen's budding sexuality. Your sweet innocent child has turned, overnight, into a hormone with feet. He has a surge in emotions, an interest in sex, and different parts of his body are growing at different rates. What is a parent to do?

PREPARE OR PANIC?

As a former Boy Scout, I have learned to apply the motto "Be Prepared" to parenting. The more prepared we are, the less we panic. Let me introduce seven helpful tips on "How to Build a Campfire." Oops! Wrong list. Here it is, "How to Survive Puberty, the Second Time":

1. *Acknowledge the differences.* Your child is going to encounter changes physically, emotionally, mentally, and socially. Don't live in denial. Acknowledge that these are happening and that they are normal and natural. Don't call too much attention to them, though. Saying "Wow! I can't believe how *huge* your feet are!" is not recommended.
2. *Anticipate the changes.* Be positive and look to the future. Don't act surprised or disappointed when your preteen (or early teenager) hits puberty. Your goal is to get him or her to look down the road with hope and anticipation. Your teen will pick up on your emotional state. If you are stressed and anxious about his puberty; chances are he will be, too.
3. *Talk about the changes.* Make puberty an approved topic of conversation at your house. When appropriate,

91

talk about your own journey through puberty, and
how you dealt with the challenges and changes (more
about this later).

4. *Accept the whole range of emotions.* Emotions are
   like a box of crayons. When your child was younger,
   she had the 8-pack. There wasn't a lot of variety.
   When your child hits puberty, she instantly gets a 64-
   pack of emotions—emotions of every tone, hue, and
   color. Accept and affirm each of these emotions.
   Some will be easier to accept than others. If your
   teenager feels that you accept her, and her extensive
   palette of emotions, she will be more likely to talk
   with you about her life. If she feels you only want the
   "happy kid," then she will only try to connect with
   you when she is happy. Emotions aren't right or
   wrong, they are signals of what is going on within
   the heart.
5. *Acknowledge the sexual pressure he or she faces.*
   Teens are facing more and more pressure at younger
   ages to be sexually active. Let your teen know you
   understand the pressure. Let him know you are open
   to talk about it when he wants to.
6. *Guide your teen to develop sexual standards and
   goals.* Your child has never been an adolescent before. This is foreign territory for her. You can serve as
   a guide by helping your teen develop personal values
   and commitments (more on this in the next chapter).
7. *Maintain a sense of humor.* There will be many opportunities to laugh and smile. Do it! Some of the
   funniest stories I have heard have come from the perils of puberty. Don't get too uptight. There will be
   times to be serious, just don't try to make a serious issue out of something that is destined to be humorous.

There you have it—seven tips on how to survive puberty the second time. Don't you wish your parents had these?

Though adolescence is a stressful time, it can be filled with laughs as well; remember to maintain that sense of humor (Point 7). One mother told me that she couldn't figure out why her family had been going through so much milk. She later discovered her son drinking about a half gallon a day. She asked him why he was drinking so much. "Because I'm thirsty," he responded.

He kept this up for weeks. The mother probed some more. Finally, the thirteen year-old admitted his plan, "Mom, I'm drinking so much milk because I want to get bigger."

"Oh, you mean like those milk commercials on TV?"

"No."

Perplexed, the mother inquired, "What do you mean bigger?"

"Well . . ." the boy hesitated, "I want to get a bigger chest—you know, pectorals. I have been doing push-ups and drinking milk."

"Why so much?"

"Umm," he stammered with embarrassment, "when you were pregnant with the baby, you got *huge* breasts, 'cause you were nursing and everything. I figured if I had that much milk in me I'd get a huge chest. "

The mother smiled, and tried not to laugh. Now, years later, she and her son enjoy the humor of the story.

TWO DEVELOPMENTAL TASKS

When our children hit puberty, there are two primary tasks that they need to be able to do if they are going to navigate this stage of life: 1. Accept their changing bodies and learn to control them. 2. Accept themselves as sexual beings and find their satisfying social roles as young men and women. Here's how we parents can help them with each of these tasks.

1. Accepting a changing body and learning how to use it effectively.

One of the most obvious changes in a developing

adolescent is physical. The physical changes at adolescence cause a teen to reevaluate his perception of himself physically. *Where am I in comparison to my peers? Am I taller? Shorter? Thinner? Heavier? Am I more mature? Am I behind everyone in my development?*

Typically, teens do not see themselves as ranking as high as their peers in strength and beauty. Regardless of how they feel, they are stuck with their new bodies. Some may feel like they won a contest, while others may feel ripped off.

The self-concept that they had prior to puberty will be challenged. It may interfere with accepting their new physical appearance and image. For instance, many young teenage girls are disappointed with their loss of strength and coordination that they had just months before puberty. Chances are, it will return, but for a season they may mourn the loss of "how fast I could throw a softball." Or they may say, "I used to be able to beat that boy in a race, now he beats me."

As parents, we need to help our children learn to accept their new bodies and learn to use them effectively. Being patient, giving instruction, and sending positive nonverbal messages will help your teen feel more comfortable with her new body.

2. *Accepting oneself as a sexual being and achieving a satisfying masculine or feminine social role.*

At age nine, a boy will ignore girls or tease them. He doesn't tease them because he likes them; he teases them because girls "bug" him. When that same boy hits puberty, he begins to tease girls so they will notice him. He notices their beautiful hair, the shape of their legs, and their fragrant smell. Everything about them is fascinating. Girls used to repel him, now they are like a magnet to him. The boy is discovering sexuality.

Adolescents have the task of developing a workable notion of themselves sexually, as male or as female. This will affect how they look at themselves; how they relate to members of the opposite sex; their view of love and sex; and it will influence decisions they make regarding their sexuality.

Parents can help their teens with this developmental task. We can speak openly about masculine and feminine roles. We can model our own acceptance and security with our role and with our sexuality. Help your teen understand messages, like: *I like being a male.* Or, *It's fun being a woman.*

We can give our teens hope by talking about our own journey through puberty. Let them know that what may seem overwhelming and confusing at times becomes clearer with time.

We can integrate our values into these discussions with our teens. Parents empower their teens to make wise decisions when they equip them with a healthy attitude toward their own sexuality.

Our teenage children will need our help to understand and handle their sexuality. Youth expert Walt Mueller explains the challenge:

> When the beautiful God-given gift of sexual maturity begins to blossom, teens go through an exciting and confusing time. Many eleven, twelve, and thirteen year-olds are physiologically capable of having intercourse. Some eleven- and twelve-year old girls can bear children, and active sperm cells are present in some boys of the same age. Both experience strong sexual urges and desires that they are tempted to satisfy. Couple that with a society that says "Go ahead and do it," and you've got emotionally immature kids making some very unwise choices. Many kids allow themselves to be controlled by their sexual thoughts and desires instead of responsibly managing their sexuality.[2]

CUSTOMIZE YOUR STRATEGY

Have you noticed that your kids are different? I don't mean weird, I just mean different from each other. They come from the same factory, but somebody switched the molds. They have different personalities, different temperaments, and different tastes. Those differences become magnified in adolescence.

Your casual, kicked-back kid turns into a messy teenager. Your active, energetic child morphs into a hyperkinetic lightening bolt. Since each child is different, we need to customize a strategy to help prepare each child for adolescence.

I was a youth pastor for fifteen years. I took care of other people's kids. I took them on trips. I was there when they made commitments to Christ. I baptized them. I helped them with problems. I dealt with everything imaginable. That is why, when my daughter approached her teenage years, I was anxious. I was afraid she might turn out like some of the kids in my youth group! And so I began asking myself several questions:

How will I help her prepare for the perils of puberty?
Will she ignore me and distance herself from me?
How can I be sure she will make wise choices?

The more I thought about Nicole's approaching adolescence, the more it unsettled me. *This is coming too fast. I am not ready for her to be a teenager yet! I have so much to do to get her ready. Where should I start?*

I made a list of the things I wanted to deal with before Nicole hit puberty. I had about fifty topics to discuss with her. I wasn't sure if I could get to all topics in time. I wasn't sure they were even the right topics. I decided to do a little research. I surveyed over five hundred young teens. (OK, maybe more than a little, but it was worth it.) I asked them on which topics would they like to have more information. I was surprised by their responses—there was an overwhelming agreement. I narrowed the responses to the thirty most requested issues. Heeding my own advice to parents, that "not every moment is a teachable moment," I decided to write Nicole letters, instead of lecture her thirty times.

I would write a letter and give it to Nicole to read. Most of the time we would discuss it. Some of the topics she wasn't interested in at twelve years old. Those same topics have become more relevant as she has become a few years older. Some of the topics I wrote about were the pressure of expectations, the emotional roller coaster, being shy, being tempted, learning to set sexual standards, and how to stay close to God.

This was my way to customize a strategy to prepare her for adolescence. Most of us dads are looking for a tool to help us prepare our daughters (and sons) for adolescence. Writing letters may be the last thing you want to do to prepare your child for puberty. There are other ways you can help prepare your son or daughter for the teen years. Consider what you are comfortable with and design a way to integrate talking with your child about the issues of puberty. It doesn't matter if he is already a teenager; you can start now.

One of my friends likes to fish. He takes his sons for a special one-on-one fishing trip. On the way to the lake, they listen to James Dobson's audiotapes on "Preparing for Adolescence." When they get to the cabin, they have plenty of time to discuss what they listened to.

The letters to Nicole led to some great discussions. Eventually some friends encouraged us to share the letters with others. With Nicole's permission, it was published in book form as *Letters to Nicole: Letters About Life and Love From a Father to His Daughter* (Tyndale). The book has become a useful tool for launching discussions in our relationship. Nicole has also used it as a ready-reference tool when she is talking about issues with her friends. She often gives it as a birthday gift.

In case you are wondering, for our second daughter, we needed to customize another approach. I couldn't just give her the book *Letters to Nicole* and tell her to read it (although I thought about it). After the book came out, I asked her, "Brooke, Nicole has this book for her. What would you like to do so I can do something special for you?"

"Dad, I don't want to read some boring non-fiction

book. Let's write a fiction book that gets the point across. That would be more interesting."

"You mean both of us?"

"Yeah, let's do it together."

And so we are. We are working on a fiction series where the heroine discovers key principles to life in the midst of her adventures. It is quite different from the approach I took with Nicole; but like I said, my kids are different. Aren't yours?

HELPING YOUR TEENS MANAGE THEIR SEXUALITY

Significantly, *Merriam-Webster's Collegiate Dictionary* discusses sexual change as it defines *puberty* as: "the condition of being or the period of becoming first capable of reproducing sexually marked by maturing of the genital organs [and] the development of secondary sex characteristics." Within that definition is the reality of ongoing sexual development. Probably one of the greatest worries for parents is that their teens will become sexually active.

Besides being disappointed, as Christian parents we realize that sexual activity before marriage would be a violation of Scripture. The apostle Paul makes it very clear that sexual urges must be brought under control: "It is God's will that you should be holy: that you should avoid sexual immorality; that each of you should learn to control his own body in a way that is holy and honorable, not in passionate lust like the heathen, who do not know God" (1 Thessalonians 4:3–5).

Their Sources of Information

Sex is a wonderfully designed gift of the Creator, intended to be enjoyed and protected within the context of marriage. This is what we desire for our teens. But with the onslaught of our child's puberty, we can get really nervous about the topic of sex. Researchers Sharon White and Richard DeBlassie comment, "Most teens want their parents to share sexual knowledge, opinions, beliefs, and attitudes with them.

Yet only 15 percent say that their parents are a major source of this information."[3]

The wise parent captures this time to help navigate his teen through puberty; guiding him or her into making wise choices. Preteens and teens have a natural curiosity about sex and the physical changes they are encountering. Parents have a built-in opportunity to talk with their kids about these critical concerns.

The reality is, most teens go elsewhere for their information on puberty and sexuality. When Christian teens were asked to rank their sources of sexual information, parents came in third, after friends and movies! School classes and television tied with parents.[4] Our teens are being exposed to sexual misinformation without the guidance they need.

Some parents are afraid to talk with their teens about sex. They reason, *If we talk with them about sex, they are more likely to become sexually active.* But one medical doctor disagrees. He writes:

> Medical studies indicate that if you talk to your kids about sex, they are *less* likely, not more likely, to engage in intercourse at a young age. That's okay. Maybe you're shy, or you don't believe the studies, or you don't know what to say, or you're afraid your kids will think you foolish. Here's what you do: Find a book about sex that you feel is appropriate for your child and contains the sort of things you would like her to know. Leave it on top of your night stand for about a week. I guarantee you, it will be read! I call it Sex Education for the Squeamish.[5]

Their Need for Our Understanding and Involvement

Hopefully, we will be able to be more interactive than that. But his point is valid: we must help our children to understand. We must be involved. Many of us are not sure where to start, or what to say. We don't have role models on how to talk with our teen about puberty and sexuality; our parents said little. Yet we need to give them facts and values relating to their sexuality.

Our children need more than information and values concerning their sexuality, however. They also need help in understanding all the weird things that are happening to their body. They need help comprehending puberty.

Middle school kids are very self-conscious. They measure themselves against the standard and feel that they are too tall, too short, too big, too little, too developed, or too immature. They worry about their shoe size, their breast size, their acne, and their muscles.

Parents can have an influence on their teens. They can help them understand and prepare for the challenges of puberty and adolescence. Remember, the medical studies show that teens who come from families where parents are absent, detached, or don't talk about these issues are far more likely to engage in premarital sex.

Sheila's Story

I think of Sheila. She tried to win the love and attention of her father, but he seemed to be distant and aloof to her. When she turned fifteen, she met a boy from school and began a relationship with him. It quickly became very physical. Sheila and Tom began having sex two or three times a week.

"I think he was just using me," she confessed.

"Did you love him?" I asked.

"It is real blurry. I'm not sure what was lust and what was love."

"How did you feel after sex?"

"Used and cheap. I felt like a slut."

"I wouldn't call that love," I suggested.

"Yeah, you're right; neither would I."

"So, why did you do it?"

"For the first time in my life, I felt loved and accepted."

What would have happened if Shiela's dad was able to show her love and attention? Would it have turned out differently if her dad had taken time to talk with her about some of the critical issues of adolescence? What would have happened if he would have said to her, "Sheila, I love you," and given her a hug when she turned fifteen?

Researchers Merton and Irene Strommen have found a strong correlation between family closeness and high moral standards: "Adolescents in a close family unit are the ones most likely to say 'no' to drug use, premarital sexual activity, and other antisocial and alienating behaviors. They are also the ones most likely to adopt high moral standards."[6]

I realize that talking to our kids about puberty and sexuality can be frightening. As parents, we are not sure we will do a very good job. After all, our parents didn't do a very good job. But we can be the transitional generation. We can be the generation that starts a new tradition: the tradition of preparing our children for adolescence. It might just be what saves our kids.

How can we keep our teens from drowning in the sweeping currents of their sexuality? By talking with them about it.

CONVERSATIONS ABOUT PUBERTY AND SEX

When you give your teen an understanding of puberty, sexual knowledge, and healthy attitudes, you empower him to make wise decisions. Teens learn best when they are provided an example and an opportunity to dialogue.

Guidelines for Talking About Sex

If you are now ready (despite those uncomfortable feelings) to talk with your child about his or her sexuality, you may wonder how and when. Here are nine guidelines that spell the word *sexuality*.

S: *Starting early.* Preteens will show an interest in their changing bodies. Be open to discuss age-appropriate topics before puberty begins.

E: *Environment.* Do you appropriately display affection in the home? Do you feel safe and open to discuss sensitive topics?

X: *Example.* (I know it doesn't begin with an 'x' but it's close.) As husbands and wives, we should provide a model of pure and balanced sexuality to our teens. Are you aware of the biblical standards for sexuality? Do you practice them?

U: *Understanding.* Be aware of the words and concepts that your child will understand as you think about having the conversation. What is accurate and age-appropriate?

A: *Acceptance.* We must accept our teens as sexual beings. That means we are comfortable with their gender and relaxed when we are alone together.

L: *Loosen up.* Be relaxed, casual, and conversational. Don't lecture. Try to "go with the flow." Don't force the conversation.

I: *Initiative.* Make the first move. Take the initiative to show that you are open to talk about these issues.

T: *Time.* Take time to be gradual and natural. Be willing to be repetitive. (That is how they learn.) Be willing to use "creative redundancy."

Y: *Yield.* Yield to another time if you sense resistance or a loss of interest. Don't work toward closure. By leaving the conversation open-ended, it is easier to start it the next time.

What to Talk About

Now that you know how to talk with your teen; the question hits your brain: *What do we talk about?*

Let's return to our discussion on parenting as discipleship (chapter 3). If discipleship means "an intimate, personal relationship designed for growth and learning through imitation, dialogue, and observation," how does a parent disciple his or her child on the topic of sexuality?

I would think that one of the critical factors should be conversations about God's design for human beings. Help your preteen or teen understand some of the key biblical ideas:

1. Your body is custom designed by God (Psalm 139:13–15).
2. Your body isn't your own, it is God's temple (1 Corinthians 6:18–20).
3. Keep the temple pure and clean (2 Timothy 2:22; Hebrews 13:4).
4. Be prepared to be challenged for taking a stand for purity (1 Peter 4:1–5).
5. God's way is a way of blessings and no regrets (Ephesians 5:25–33).

You could choose one of those Scripture passages and discuss how it relates to your teen's sexuality. Just do one at a time; that will give you five conversations.

You could write out one Scripture and a letter to your daughter describing how you hope this verse will become a reality in her life.

If you know calligraphy, use this skill to artfully capture the scripture. Print or write in distinctive script on quality paper, perhaps poster size. Then surprise your teen with this special gift. Explain why the verse is important to you.

Consider doing a Bible study together of these five passages. Arrange a time and then go out for ice cream afterward. Make it fun.

Don't worry if you are a little nervous about talking with your teen about puberty. You don't have to be Dr. Ruth before you can be helpful. Contrary to the winds of our time, we don't have to be completely comfortable about sex in order to have meaningful conversations with our teens. In the next chapter, I will help you prepare to actually talk about love, sex, and dating with your teenager.

You might want to take a break and fix yourself some soothing herbal tea.

For "Almost Cool" Parents

1. What are some things that made you panic when your teen hit puberty?
2. Look over the seven tips on "How to Survive Puberty the Second Time." Which of these might most help you to handle the hormone hurricane: (1) anticipating or talking about the changes, (2) accepting their emotions, (3) maintaining your sense of humor, or (4) something else?
3. "Adolescents have the life stage task of developing a workable notion of themselves sexually—as male or as a female. This will affect how they look at themselves." How can a parent help his teen to develop healthy sexual and social roles?
4. Studies indicate that if parents talk with their kids about sex, the teens are less likely, not more likely, to engage in sexual intercourse. How do you feel about talking to your teen about such sensitive topics?
5. What are some creative ways to help teens understand that their body is God's temple (1 Corinthians 6:18–20)?

Chapter 7
TALKING ABOUT LOVE,
SEX, AND DATING

Our children are observant; they notice how people are different. I learned this early in my fathering experience. I had taken our three-year-old Brooke to the grocery store. She was in one of those inquisitive moods. She was alert to all the potential discoveries in the world. She was fascinated with human anatomy.

As we walked up and down the aisles, she announced her observations, "Daddy, that woman is *fat!*" She said it a little too loud.

"Oh look, honey," I replied, trying to distract her, "here is some macaroni and cheese" (her favorite).

On the cereal aisle she gaped at another innocent customer. "Daddy, that man is *bald!*"

The man turned and scowled at me. (As if I could do something!)

Sometimes as parents we can feel awkward—no, make that embarrassed. But Brooke is like a lot of kids—they notice and comment on what they notice. Most children also notice certain sexual differences between women and men, sometimes at the beach, other times at the store or at home. They may even mention those differences to you, declaring a great discovery. But it's often announced as mere information, not as a request to talk about sex.

TALKING ABOUT SEX: A PARENT'S PRIVILEGE AND RESPONSIBILITY

In most cases, you will have to be the one to bring up the topic of sex. From the previous chapter, it should be clear that we need to talk with our teens about puberty and sexuality. But once again you may feel awkward or embarrassed. When it comes to talking to your teen about sex, love, and dating, I know what many of you are thinking: *Why can't I let the school teach my teen? Don't they have sex education?* Or maybe you think the church should do it: *How about if I let the youth pastor teach my kid about sex?*

Nine Reasons for Parents to Talk About It

But it is the parents' responsibility and *privilege* to talk with their teens about love, sex, and dating. Consider these nine reasons:

1. No one knows your teen like you do.
2. No one loves your teen as much as you do.
3. Teens learn more from modeling and following our example than from any other method of learning. Living is more powerful than just lecturing.
4. A loving marital relationship is more than sex: it is affection, patience, sacrifice, understanding, and romance. This is best modeled in the home.
5. Sexuality is best understood in a context of a long-term committed relationship, as in marriage.
6. Teens receive a lot of misinformation about love, sex, and dating. Talking with your teens can correct and protect them, and it can inform you about their fears and misinformation.
7. Communication is essential to showing love. When

you are open to talking about a difficult topic, you are demonstrating love. Your lack of comfort and confidence may be a gift. Your teenager probably feels the same way. You can empathize with each other.

8. God has designed the home to be a place of learning about love and sexuality.

9. This conversation is one more way you prepare your children to make wise choices. Sexual activity among teens is high. We need to prepare our teens to make moral decisions that they alone can make. We can't make the choices for them, but we can prepare them to make the best choices.

Have I convinced you? Do you feel those are enough reasons to talk with your teen about a topic that might make you sweat? If not, consider this report carried by the Associated Press:

> "Most high school students have had sex," according to a survey released in 1992 by the Centers for Disease Control. Of the 11,631 high schoolers [in the survey], grades 9–12, 54% say they have had sexual intercourse.
>
> "We're particularly concerned about the increase at each grade level," said Dr. Lloyd Kolbe, director of CDC Division of Adolescent and School Health.
>
> Among ninth graders, 40% have had sex, at 10th grade, 48%. By 11th grade 57% have had sexual intercourse, and by 12th grade it's 72%. Researchers believe that high school students weren't nearly as sexually active in earlier generations.[1]

Helping Our Teens in the Adventure Called Adolescence

Many teens are having sex. Is your teen prepared to resist the sexual pressure?

We took time to prepare our kids for their first day of school. We bought them new clothes. We purchased a new lunchbox, with just the right cartoon figure. We talked to them about what might go on at school. Chances are, we walked them around the school and oriented them before school was in session. We wanted to prepare our child for his or her first day at school.

When our children approach adolescence, do we take as much effort to prepare them for their first days? Do we talk with them about their new body? Do we open discussion about their new equipment (their emerging sexual organs and gender characteristics)? How do we walk them around and orient them to puberty?

Or do we let them figure adolescence out on their own?

As we noted in chapter 6, our teens are undergoing massive personal changes and placed in totally unfamiliar territory.

Imagine being blindfolded and put on a plane to a distant continent. On the trip, you are fed strange food by unseen people who speak an unknown language. Upon arriving, you are escorted to a taxi and taken to a downtown section of a huge city. You are still wearing your blindfold. You hear bizarre sounds, but you don't recognize them. Suddenly, someone spins you around several times and quickly removes your blindfold. Dizzily, you turn to see who it is, but the blinding light from an oncoming semitrailer scares you. You are standing in the middle of a busy street! You have no idea where you are. You have no clue how to talk with the people around you. You are not sure what to do or where to go.

If you can imagine yourself in that scenario, you may be able to recapture what it feels like to be an adolescent. Unescorted and at times overwhelmed, our teens feel like aliens. That's why they need us to help them to navigate the perils of puberty and even to enjoy the adventures of adolescence.

TALKING ABOUT THE CRITICAL ISSUES

Making Time for Your Teens

As you prepare for your conversation, let me encourage you with two truths: (1) Your children want to talk with you about important issues such as their sexuality, and (2) the Scriptures give you the authority to talk about the critical issues of their lives. Youth pastor and parent educator Scott Talley says teens need parents to be role models and times to talk with them:

> Some parents feel that their teens don't want to talk with them and should be left alone. This is not accurate. *Early adolescents need strong relationships with their parents* and positive role modeling from them. From their same sex parents adolescents need to learn appropriate roles—how to be men or women. And in their relationships with opposite sex parents they prepare to relate to a future mate. So early adolescence is a time when children need their parents to make time for them and their activities. It is a tragic mistake for parents to believe the myth that teens no longer desire or need to spend time with their parents. While it is true teens are beginning to make strong peer relationships, it is not true that they do not want a relationship with their parents. Rebellious children are usually those who are reacting to poor relationships, either between their parents and themselves, or between the parents themselves. Most experts agree that rebellion is one of the primary causes of sexual promiscuity and experimentation by early adolescents [italics added].[2]

What Scripture Says

According to Scripture, parents are to be the ones who talk with their children about critical issues. Consider the commands of Deuteronomy 11:18–19: "Fix these words of mine in your hearts and minds; tie them as symbols on your hands and bind them on your foreheads. Teach them to your children, talking about them when you sit at home and when you walk along the road, when you lie down and when you get up."

Read that Bible verse again. Let me ask you: does that sound religious? Does it sound churchy? It seems rather normal to me. Talking. Sitting. Walking. Going to bed. Getting up. Sounds pretty natural to me.

We don't have to be Bible scholars to talk with our teens about love and sex. We don't have to be psychologists. We just have to *make it natural.*

Did you catch that? Our conversations about love and sex need to be woven into the normal happenings of the day. When it comes to conversations about love and sex, *we need to tie them in with the flow of life.*

This is the best way to teach children and teens. Let's say you are walking your dog around the block with your eleven-year-old daughter. Your male dog sees an attractive female poodle on the other side of the street. The beautiful dame is unescorted. Your dog pulls the leash out of your daughter's hand and darts across the street. Before you can do anything, they have sniffed, met and—horrors!—your dog is mounting the pinkish fur ball.

What will you do? Chances are, your daughter will raise a question. Are you prepared for a response? Or do you ignore it and continue walking?

Teaching Through Daily Encounters

The biblical principle seems to suggest that you seize every opportunity to teach important truths by illustrating them with natural occurrences that you encounter in your normal day.

I find this to be very liberating. A more formal and didactic approach makes me nervous. Besides, we might be presenting material our kid could care less about. I think the balance is in being prepared to talk about certain topics, should we have the opportunity and our teen's interest.

Take another look at the scripture from Deuteronomy 11. A project that I like to assign parents is to list the meaning of each biblical phrase and describe one way you could apply each principle in a realistic conversation with your teen about love and sex. Review the chart on page 111 and see if you can complete it; look for meaning and application ideas for each phrase.

Walking, talking, sitting, and eating. These are activities we are familiar with; they don't sound too scary. We can use these normal activities to introduce topics we want to

---

Chart 5
TEACH YOUR CHILDREN WELL

Here's an exercise that can help and encourage you in teaching your children. Read again Deuteronomy 11:18– 19. Then write the meaning of the phrase and an application for your own life. The first phrase has been done as an example.

Phrase	Meaning	Application
Fix these words of mine in your hearts and minds.	I need to know God's Word.	I will read it daily.
Tie them as symbols on your hands and bind them on your foreheads.		
Teach them to your children, talking about them when you sit at home.		
When you walk along the road.		
When you lie down.		
When you get up.		

---

discuss with our teenagers. Barry and Carol St. Clair suggest a couple ways we parents can do this:

> Use mealtimes to talk. Plan carefully for those mealtimes when all of you will be together. Prepare a good meal. Turn off the TV and take the phone off the hook. Begin the meal with a blessing. After the food goes around the table, ask each person to share what happened during the day. Begin with a different person each time so the talkers don't dominate. As each one talks, ask lots of questions. This keeps the conversation going, and soon everyone gets into the habit of talking to each other. As parents you stay informed, and your children build relational skills in manners, listening, and sensitivity to others. All of these help proper communication.[3]

NINE TIPS FOR EFFECTIVE COMMUNICATION

It has come time for you to get ready to talk with your teenager or preteen about love and sex. We will discuss *what* to talk about in a few pages; but first, let us consider *how* to talk with your teen.

1. Accept your teen's *feelings* (don't argue with her emotions, i.e., "You shouldn't feel that way.")
2. Accepting your teen doesn't mean that you are approving of her behavior.
3. Expect ambivalent attitudes and strong feelings. Don't be threatened by them.
4. Anticipate irritating behavior and unfavorable responses if your teen is tired, feeling pressure, or feeling cornered.
5. Choose the right time and place to discuss the issue.
6. Include your teen in planning a time for you to get away, have fun, and talk.
7. Communicate respect to your teen. Show value by listening.
8. Respond with care to sensitive subjects.

9. Give your teen truthful answers to his questions in an age-appropriate manner.

RICHARD'S SECRET

But what if you haven't talked, and your child already has received from others incorrect, distorted, or even perverted information about his or her sexuality? You can still have that conversation. It's not too late. Consider Richard.

Richard had a secret; to him, everything was fine until his mom found out. When she discovered his secret, she called me.

"Tim, I can't believe it. I never thought I would have to deal with this. Richard is such a normal kid."

With that kind of opening line I thought: *drugs, alcohol, runaway, or failing in school.* I asked, "What's going on with Richard?"

"I am embarrassed to tell you. I think he is a pervert. Where did I go wrong?"

"What is he doing?"

"I was cleaning today. Under his mattress. I have a hard time saying it . . . OK, I can say it: pornography! I am just so upset, I don't know what to do."

"You found some magazines hidden in his bedroom?"

"Yes, three of them, with the most disgusting pictures. I was shocked. Do you think Richard is a pervert?"

"I don't think so; a lot of fourteen-year-old boys are curious about sex."

"And this is a fine way to show it!" she exclaimed sarcastically.

"Actually, it is a fairly common way to get information about sex. Have you ever had a conversation about sex with him?"

"No. We talked about doing it, but I thought his father should."

"Did he?"

"I doubt it."

"Me too."

"Well, what should I do?"

"Get together with your husband and come up with a plan. Try to be positive and upbeat, but firm. Don't shame Richard, but let him know pornography is neither healthy nor accepted in your home."

"What do we say? I mean, how do we start?"

"After you and your husband talk, invite Richard to talk with the two of you. Make sure it is private and not rushed. Remind your son of your love for him. Let him know that if he has questions, he can come to either of you. You want to open the lines of communication. Make sure he feels that you are accessible."

"But what about the magazines?"

"That's next. Then ask Richard, 'Do you feel you can talk with us about difficult topics?' He'll probably say, 'yes.' Then say, 'OK, let's talk about these,' and produce the magazines. He'll probably be shocked, but don't put him on the defensive. That is counterproductive in the long run."

"I just want to smack him over the head with them and yell at him!"

"I know you are mad at him. You have a right to be. But try to focus the anger at the behavior, not the person. Try to respond sensitively to this sensitive subject."

"What will he say?"

"Who knows? But let him know this isn't a healthy way to get information about sex. Let him know that you will provide him with information."

"Not more magazines!"

Chuckling, I respond, "No, not more magazines. But solid, biblical information on sexuality, love, and marriage. He has a natural hunger for it."

"Don't they do that at school? Aren't you doing something at the church youth group?"

"Yes, the school does some, but they don't do it very well. Besides, I don't think we would agree with what they are teaching. And yes, we do teach biblical standards for dating and sex in the youth group; but it is primarily your responsibility to help your son learn these principles."

"Mine?"

"Yes, yours and your husband's. If you design a plan to talk with your son about love, sex, and dating, it just might help him avoid an addiction to pornography. In fact, this is an opportunity to introduce the idea. It is a natural bridge to a conversation you have wanted to have but didn't know how to start."

"This is good?"

"It can become good. It is your chance to disciple your son about one of the most critical areas in life."

"Maybe my husband could get together and discuss this stuff with Richard. I have heard of fathers doing that. It's not too early, is it?"

"What do you think?"

"I guess not. He obviously has started his own research!" she said lightly. "What should they discuss?"

"I'll send you my list. It will help them to know what to talk about."

WHAT TO TALK ABOUT

Whether your situation is like that of Richard's mom—having a late conversation about sex—or it's taking place before he has asked someone else or done his own kind of research, be sure to do *your* research before you talk with your preteen or teen. Know what you will say about the topics below (and others you may add). You will never know when the opportunity will arise to talk. Be prepared, it could happen at the weirdest times.

Take a look at the checklist on page 116. Notice the topics extend beyond your teen's sexual feelings to other aspects of puberty. Mark the topics that you need more input on. Choose the order in which you would like to discuss them with your teen or preteen. You may need to read from books specifically written on the topic. Even then, you may feel you need more information; you may want to discuss ideas with other parents.

Remember, the list below is to help you prepare for a dialogue with your teenager. Develop an order that is age-appropriate to your child. Try spending the majority of your time on those topics that are most important. If during the discussion the time is getting short or either you or your teen seems tired, wrap it up and suggest another time to continue the dialogue.

Chart 6
"What to Talk About" Checklist

Use the following list to help you talk with your teen or preteen about changes and issues during puberty.

1. Definition of puberty

2. Changes in hair, voice, muscles, skin, and body odor

3. Body size and shape

4. Menstrual periods

5. Sexual organs

6. Emotions

7. Sexual attraction

8. Masturbation

9. Pornography

10. Sexual harassment and teasing

11. Designer sex (following the plan of God, who designed sexuality and proper sexual expression; 1 Corinthians 6:16–20)

12. Sexual intercourse and virginity

13. Pregnancy

14. Sex expresses love, and commitment

15. Dangers of sex (physical and emotional)

16. Why wait for sex? (abstinence and purity)

17. Other: _____

HELPING YOUR TEEN SET SEXUAL SAFEGUARDS

I have met many teens who have not heard from their parents the facts of life, or if they have, it has not included clear practical guidelines. Don't pass up your opportunity as a parent to lay the groundwork for future conversations about love and sex. An early conversation can prevent misinformation and wrong attitudes about sex, while opening doors to later conversations your son or daughter may want to initiate.

The sixteen topics above could be part of an initial dialogue with your teen about love, sex, and dating. But be sure at some point to discuss guidelines and limits for proper sexual behavior that reflect your desire to help your teen handle sexual temptation. I remember a conversation I once had with Jason. It reminds me of how teens want to talk with their parents about sex, and it illustrates how we can give guidance when we talk to them with sensitivity and love.

Jason was a good-looking junior in our youth group. I noticed that he had started dating Erin. I ventured a conversation. "So you and Erin are going out?"

"Yeah," he smiled, "She's cool. I like her."

"What do you like about her?"

"Oh, I dunno; everything, I guess."

"What?" I persisted.

"I like her looks, she's a babe."

"Yeah she is. Good taste, man."

"Thanks, I think so," Jason paused, looked around, saw that we were alone, and asked, "Hey, Tim, can I ask you a question?"

"Sure."

"Umm . . . uh . . . I like Erin and everything. I mean, we are both Christians and all, but we really like each other. You know what I mean?"

"Yeah."

"Well, we are getting pretty physical." He looked around to make sure the conversation was still private.

"And?"

"OK, how far can we go?" He raised his eyebrows and smiled.

"Do you know what God says?"

"Yeah, no sex until you are married."

"Is the rule good or bad?"

"I suppose it's good, but it seems difficult."

"Jason, the rule isn't bad, the world is. Some people say the world is good and rules are bad, but the opposite is true. The world is an evil place, and we can get hurt if we don't follow God's rules. God's rule for sex is to protect us because He loves us."

"Kind of like our parents' rules?"

"Exactly. Our heavenly Father knew we would really get hurt and mess things up if we had sex outside of marriage. Can you think of some examples?"

"Plenty. I can think of lots of kids who only got hurt because they got involved sexually. We don't want to go all the way. How far can we go before we are sinning?"

"The Bible emphasizes purity, not specific acts. That is because for one guy, holding hands might be all he can handle; for another guy he might be able to handle a kiss or even a hug without getting carried away with lust."

"Yeah, I know what you mean. It depends on the situation." He paused, grinned and continued, "It depends on the girl!"

"You are right. What goes on in your head is just as important as what goes on with your hands. Here's a verse for you: 'Don't let anyone look down on you because you are young, but set an example for the believers in speech, in life, in love, in faith and in purity.' It's in 1 Timothy 4:12."

"So purity is the big thing."

"Yes. The question isn't *How far can you go?* The question is *How can I show purity in my relationship with Erin?*"

"That's a totally different way to look at it."

"It may not be the most popular, but I think that is what Scripture is teaching."

"OK, I think I understand the why behind the rule; but I still need some specifics."

"All right, I have five pointers. I wish I got a buck for every time someone asked me about this."

"You mean, I'm not alone?" He glanced around to see if anyone had walked up.

"No, you are not alone. I get asked this all the time."

"Cool," he said with a huge smile.

"First, hand-holding, quick hugs, and sitting close to each other are good ways to express how you feel without getting yourselves into trouble. Second, kissing too long and French kissing can steam things up pretty quickly. If you find yourself fantasizing about the next step, you have kissed too long. Third, don't lie down beside each other, especially if no one else is around, or if you are wearing your swimsuits. That is just too tempting!"

"You are right about that," agreed my interested teen-age friend.

"Fourth, caressing or touching each other on the breasts or in the genital area is one guaranteed way to lose control. Save that for marriage. That is called foreplay and it is de-signed to get you ready for sex. Finally, don't be alone with Erin in her home or yours, without your parents around. Stay out of parked cars and tempting situations. Sometimes, if we are in the wrong environment, our impulses drive us much farther than our godly intentions."

"Hey, thanks, Tim. That really helped. I wish I could talk to my folks like I can talk with you."

Our teens *should* be able to talk to us parents. Teen-agers are looking for conversations like this one. As Jason's youth pastor, I had the privilege of having the conversation with him. But here is my encouragement to you, dear parent: It is a privilege to talk with your children about love and sexuality.

Don't miss out on an opportunity to connect with your teenage children on this critical topic.

Believe it or not, you can influence your teenager. A national research study of 710 teenagers, conducted by the Barna Research Group, supports this.

> They may not like to admit it openly, but teenagers do realize that they are greatly influenced by their family. In fact, when asked to describe the individuals who exert the greatest degree of influence upon them, family members lead the pack; mother, then father, with siblings not far behind.[4]

That is encouraging, isn't it! If we can influence our teens, what more important topic than love, sex, and dating?

For "Almost Cool" Parents

1. Consider the "Nine Reasons for Parents to Talk" about love, sex, and dating. Which of the reasons do you agree with the most? The least?
2. According to Deuteronomy 11:18–19, parents are to be the ones who talk with their children about critical issues. What are some creative ways we can apply this Scripture passage to our contemporary parenting? (Refer to Chart 5 for ideas.)
3. Read the "Nine Tips for Effective Communication" on pages 112–13. Give yourself a grade—A, B, C, or D—for each. Then ask, "What can I do to raise my GPA (great parenting average)?" Discuss your answer.
4. Explain your priorities for discussion from the "What to Talk About Checklist" you completed.
5. What do you think about the conversation with Jason? What would you have told Jason?

Chapter 8
EMPOWERING YOUR TEEN: RIGHT VALUES AND ENCOURAGEMENT

I have written a book entitled *The Relaxed Parent*. I get teased about it.

"That's an oxymoron if I ever heard one."

"Must be a fiction book. Ha, ha, ha!"

"You must not have any children, certainly not teenagers."

Those comments warm my soul. Those of us living, breathing, semi-comatose parents of teens know one thing about adolescence: It is a living paradox. Teenagers are oxymoronic within themselves. At times, they are simply moronic.

Sometimes it is impossible to comprehend teenagers. They often don't understand themselves. As author and family counselor Gordon Porter Miller writes:

> The normal [high school teenager] is a *living paradox*. Teenagers reflect a variety of seemingly contradictory attitudes and characteristics. They are both:
>
> • impulsive and thoughtful
> • shy and confident

- rude and sensitive
- daring and cautious
- individualistic and conforming
- arrogant and timid
- tough and scared
- omnipotent-feeling and powerless
- mature and childish

It's no wonder parents anticipate these years with anxiety and fear, and it's easy to see why they so often feel exasperated. Suddenly, a whole bunch of conflict-charged situations arise. Issues relating to teenage sexuality, preparation for college or work, the first car, financial independence, and treatment as a young adult virtually explode into the family setting.[1]

A teenager may swear at her parents, storm out of the room, and slam her bedroom door, frightening the cat. Her rudeness can change in an instant to sensitivity. "Oh, Fluffy! I'm so sorry I scared you. Come here, precious."

Meanwhile, the parents are in the living room trying to recover from the verbal assault.

One of my favorite pubescent paradoxes (try saying that fast three times!) is the individualistic-versus-conforming tension. Consider this conversation in the mall:

Teen: "I just want to be myself. I want to dress in a way that is 'me.'"

Parent: "Then why not wear these beige slacks. That would be different."

Teen: "I don't want to be *that* different. That is weird!"

Parent: "So what do you want?"

Teen: "I want to express myself. I want to experience freedom."

Parent: "So you want to be yourself?"

Teen: "Yeah. Finally, you are getting it."

Parent: "I understand. You want to be unique but not too different."

Teen: "Yeah," she says, looking around. "Here, look at these," holding up baggy pants. "These are soooo cool!"

Parent: "They look just like what the two thousand other teens in the mall are wearing."

Teen: "No. These are different. They are *gray!* Those others are black, or navy blue. These are cool because they are gray. Now that's different! And look at the coin pocket; the stitching is totally different!"

Parent: "You should really stand out wearing those."

Teen: (proudly) "With these, I can be myself," displaying the pants.

Parent: (thinking) *You'll look like a clone of the other kids.*

Sound familiar? Have you seen examples of the *living paradox* in your teen's behavior?

PASSING ON VALUES

Despite the confusing, contradictory times, your teen needs and wants you. And you can empower him to become a maturing individual—a responsible adult—by passing on your values and encouraging your teen as he changes and matures.

How do we pass on what's important to us? First, decide what *your* values are. What is most important to you? For me, they are honesty, faith, autonomy, and compassion. These are the virtues I want to see developed in my teens' lives.

Once you know what is important to you, verbally communicate these values to your teen. Say something like this:

"I want to help you establish honesty as the foundation for all your relationships. I want your faith in God to be at the center of your life. I will do all I can to help you learn how important it is to be independent, but also compassionate. Are you interested in learning these things?"

Develop a Plan

Wait for a response. See if you can develop a plan with your teen to cultivate those qualities in her life. Some parents have found it helpful to make a list of behaviors that will help them measure if they and their teen are moving toward these qualities. For example, "Darlene will be home by midnight on weekend evenings, or will call by 11:30 P.M. to notify me of her situation, location, and plans." This kind of specific behavior defined and written will clarify expectations. Parents can also introduce the concept of the value they are seeking to develop. In this case, it could be consideration. "We demonstrate consideration to others when we let them know where we are and when we come home on time."

Consideration is more important than the curfew. As a parent, you may be negotiable on the curfew if your teen takes the time to call and keep you posted.

Nicole's Plan

This is what we do with Nicole. She doesn't have a curfew. She is proud to tell her friends that, too! Actually, she does have a curfew; we negotiate it every time she goes out. In my youth ministry experience, I discovered teens who had curfews at midnight, but nothing worthwhile to do from 10 P.M. to twelve. They usually got into trouble. If the situation warrants it, your teen may need more time. In some cases, a teen will need less time.

Under our arrangement, if Nicole is out with friends and needs more time, she calls. We usually grant her more time if:

- she is with friends we know and trust
- she is at a place that we feel secure about
- she is caught up on her sleep and not grumpy

- she has something legitimate to do that warrants an extension of time
- she doesn't have early commitments in the morning

This arrangement has helped us to dialogue and set reasonable limits with our daughter. Actually, the discussion and the assessment of time might be more beneficial than a set-in-stone curfew. Teens are motivated to dialogue with their parents if they get something out of it. In this case, they are negotiating for more time.

ENCOURAGE AND CONFRONT

Look for ways to affirm your teen every time you see him or her doing something right. This includes anything the teen is doing that is moving him in the right direction, whether he successfully accomplishes the behavior or not. Emphasize progress more than perfection.

Confront your teen when he is doing something wrong (anything that leads him away from the goals you have mutually agreed upon). Let him/her know that wrong behavior is disappointing and hurtful to you. I think it is helpful to pause after sharing this. For example:

"Son, you have been negligent with your chores around the house. I am disappointed in your behavior." Pause. Let your teen feel your disappointment; create some tension by waiting longer than you would normally. (Teens hate this. That is why I am suggesting it! It's a form of discipline.)

"This kind of behavior not only hurts me, but it can hurt you. It will have an effect on you." Again, pause. Let the consequence of lost privileges and freedom sink in. Ask, "What can *we* do about this?"

Listen to your teen suggest corrective measures. By allowing your son to think through these, you are demonstrating trust. You are building into his life the virtues of trust and personal responsibility.

Be consistent in fulfilling your end of the deal. If you

have agreed to allow your teen certain privileges in return for certain behavior, keep your word.

Encourage your teen to use his or her values to make his or her own decisions. Remind your teen that he already makes most of his decisions. Establishing healthy values will help him make wiser decisions.

I like to tell teens, "Decide on your values, stick to them, and use them to make wise decisions. Otherwise, others will make your decisions for you."

"What do you mean by that?" they ask.

"There will always be a person around who likes to take control of your life. He likes to tell you what to do. If you don't know ahead of time what is important to you, this person often winds up telling you what to do, and you do it. If you want control of your life, decide on your values, commit yourself to them and use them to make your decisions. If you let others make your decisions for you, and they may make stupid ones, then you really lose. Then someone else runs your life, usually some authority—police, juvenile hall officer, the principal, etc."

To assist in passing on values to your teen, help him evaluate his values in light of Scripture. If your teen cannot find support in the Bible for one of his values, encourage him to reevaluate it (and change it).

ENCOURAGE, DON'T EXASPERATE

Encourage, encourage, encourage any effort to live by biblical values, even if the effort is mediocre. Remember, *progress, not perfection.*

At my parenting seminars, I like to ask, "See if you can complete the following statement: "If it is worth doing it is . . .""

Parents always reply, "it is worth doing well, or not at all."

"Where did you learn this?" I ask them. "You all responded in unison. You must have had the same parents! Look around the room, meet your long-lost brothers and sisters!

Isn't that interesting, you all were able to complete the phrase with the same saying. Where did you learn this?"

Usually, the response is, "From my parents."

I gently, and with great diplomacy, say, "Your parents were *wrong!*"

"It's Worth Doing Poorly"

I observe their shocked or agitated faces, then continue, "Think about it. If something is worth doing—if it has inherent worth in doing it—it is worth doing poorly. If it is worth doing, any attempt at it is going in the right direction. It doesn't have to be perfect for it to have value. Sometimes we can't learn to do something well unless we try and learn from trial and error. *If it is worth doing, it's worth doing poorly!"*

I know this bothers you perfectionists. But if our teens are going to learn values, we need to give them some training wheels. We need to let them have a few crashes and a few bandaged knees. It is better for them to learn while they are under our protection and watchful eye than to have to learn in the big, bad world when they are on their own. The home is the place where they can learn without the full impact of negative consequences. They can learn from trial and error, without being devastated.

Probably one of the most influential ways to pass on your values is to understand the principle: *Encourage, don't exasperate.* Encourage means to "pour courage into someone." It means to give the person strength that he doesn't have in himself. Teens need encouragement. Adolescence is overwhelming to them. When we encourage our teens we are meeting one of their greatest emotional needs. With this met, they are more likely to catch our values. As the Scripture wisely counsels, "Fathers [and mothers], do not exasperate your children; instead, bring them up in the training and instruction of the Lord" (Ephesians 6:4).

Exasperate means to "enrage, annoy or irritate." Parents exasperate their teens when they expect too much. When they expect perfection. When they expect them to learn something the first try. We irritate our teens when we expect them to respond like adults.

Be on His Side

Your teen is more likely to adopt your values if he feels you are on his side. We can't even get to the "training and instruction of the Lord" part if we short-circuit the process by exasperating our teens.

We hear a lot about "family values." What would you say are your family's top three values, and how do you teach and transfer each to your teen? Here's a way to determine that. Take out a piece of paper and make three columns. Write your family's top three values on the left-hand side. In the middle, describe how you are currently modeling or teaching each value to your teen. In the third column, brainstorm with your teenagers some creative ways you could transfer each value to your teen.

For instance, one of our family values is compassion. In the second column (the one that asks, "What am I doing to teach this value?"), I could write, "By encouraging our teens to give to those in need. By being involved in service projects for the urban poor." For the new idea column, "Volunteer as a family to serve dinner to the homeless at the shelter."

I suggest that you allow your teen to give input to the new idea column. Let her in on the discussion and planning. In passing on values remember, "Values are something we do *with* our teens, not *to* our teens."

THIRTY WAYS TO ENCOURAGE YOUR TEEN

Encouragement is very important to helping our children through the turbulent teen years, especially in helping them learn and hold on to important values. Here are thirty ways you can encourage your teen through your actions and words during those changing times of adolescence.

Things to Do

1. Ask him or her to help on a project you'd both enjoy.
2. Ask for his or her opinion.
3. Delegate the planning of a family day or vacation to your teen.
4. Do something together to help someone in need.
5. Ask for his perspective on current events.
6. Buy her favorite candy or snack and surprise her with it.
7. Ask her what you can pray about for her.
8. Go to an athletic event together.
9. Go to a concert together.
10. Attend the recital, debate, play, or sporting event in which your teen is involved.
11. Include her in the next conversation with your adult friends.
12. Dream with him about his future (don't give direction, just imagine).
13. Go out for a "date" together (dinner, movie, batting cages, etc.).
14. Write your teen a note and mail it. Tell him what you like about him.
15. Spend a half day doing whatever *your teen* wants to do.

Things to Say

1. "You were thoughtful when . . ."
2. "I have confidence in you."
3. "You make sense."
4. "You are really maturing."
5. "What I like about you is (name a quality)."
6. "That is a unique way of looking at things."
7. "What suggestion would you like to make?"
8. "It's OK to feel that way."

9. "Sometimes, I feel the same way." (Give an example.)
10. "I can see improvement in the area of . . ."
11. "Thanks for being yourself. I like being around you."
12. "You really seem to be learning from your mistakes."
13. "I was wrong. Will you forgive me?"
14. "I love you."
15. "You are one of a kind."

Take another look at these thirty suggestions. Pick one thing to do and one thing to say that are new. Practice these with your teen this week. Don't worry about failure. Don't worry about doing them right the first time. Remember, "If it's worth doing, it's worth doing" (even with mediocrity!).

During her Christmas vacation one year, my Nicole was sick. Talk about being discouraged—vacation and feeling sick. Suzanne called me at work and suggested I bring home flowers for her. To be honest, I would have never thought to bring her flowers. I'm glad my wife called. I brought home a bouquet of roses, and Nicole was thrilled.

"No one has ever brought me roses! Thanks, Dad!" She gave me a huge hug.

I didn't even mind the germs. She thanked me five times for the roses. She mentioned how beautiful they looked three times. I had no idea they would have that much impact on her. I was excited to discover a meaningful way to encourage my teenage daughter.

BARRIERS TO EMPOWERING YOUR TEEN

I have observed four barriers that keep parents from empowering their teens. If empowering a teenager means to "build into and let go," these four may explain why some parents have difficulty.

1. A Negative Bias Toward Teens

Some parents are suspicious about all teens, not just their teens. They assume, *They are up to no good.* This form of prejudice does not lead to the trust that is necessary for empowerment. Parents with this bias focus on the negative traits of adolescent behavior and do not see those things that are praiseworthy.

I think some of the bias occurs because it is much easier to observe obnoxious behavior than it is mature behavior. A typical parent with this bias might read in the paper about "The Growing Menace of Drugs." Later that day, he may see some teens "loitering" and assume that they are involved in drugs.

Another aspect of this negative bias is what I call "Exploded Experience." A parent with this bias may have a negative encounter with his or her own teen; he or she then "explodes" this experience to be representative of all adolescents. You know this is happening when you hear comments like: "Teenagers—you can't trust them!" and "All they want is sex, drugs, and rock 'n roll."

2. A Loss of Connection Between Separate Worlds

Some teens live in a teen-only world with parents who haven't helped them bridge the gap into the adult world. Some parents don't value the teen world, and they want nothing to do with it. They don't attempt to understand or involve themselves with this "foreign" world. As a result, teens feel alienated from the people who brought them into the world—their parents. That could explain some of the feelings of betrayal teens often experience.

3. Seeing Teens as Consumers Rather Than Contributors

Teens are demanding, but they are also capable of giving. When we only see our kids as takers, they tend to live down to that expectation. In too many homes teens are never asked to contribute to the work or the economy of the family.

They don't understand that they are active members of a community. Members of a community contribute.

Parents with this perception have falsely believed that they need to give their teens "time to be kids." By doing this, they are robbing their teens of self-worth, self-confidence, and feelings of significance. We rob our teens of meaning when we don't expect them to work for the common good of the family. Teens need to be treated as members, not guests.

4. Not Understanding Progressive Release

I know the phrase "progressive release" may sound like a gymnastics term. "She has really mastered the high bar in this Olympics. Note her 'progressive release,' Jim!"

Progressive release is a term I use to describe the road toward independence. It is the gradual process a teen goes through to become autonomous and self-sufficient. Some parents don't understand this. Because they don't, they stand in the way of their teens growing up and being capable adults. Sure, your teen may leave home when he is eighteen, but is he able to take care of himself, provide for himself, and make wise decisions?

This principle is biblical. That is why it is important that we understand it and remove this barrier from empowering our teen. Jesus described the gradual acquiring of more responsibilities:

> Whoever can be trusted with very little can also be trusted with much, and whoever is dishonest with very little will also be dishonest with much. So if you have not been trustworthy in handling worldly wealth, who will trust you with true riches? And if you have not been trustworthy with someone else's property, who will give you property of your own? (Luke 16:10–12)

As our children mature, we trust them with more. If they can handle not getting into trouble in the backyard, we let them play in the front yard. If they can handle that, they are given the freedom to roam up and down a few houses; later they earn the right to roam the neighborhood. As they prove themselves, they are given more freedom and responsibility.

If a teen can't be trusted with little, we shouldn't give him more. But some parents have a difficult time letting their teens grow up and giving them more and more freedom and responsibility as they prove they can handle it. This exasperates teens.

I like to think about a "Countdown to Independence." When our children are small, we are 100 percent responsible for them. We bathe them. We feed them. We change their clothes. But as they mature, they do more and we do less. When they become teenagers we need to start the countdown.

"You are fifteen now. When you are eighteen you will be going to college. I want you to be prepared to be on your own."

"Sounds cool, Dad. What do you mean?"

"What are some things that we do now that you should take responsibility for in the next three years?"

"Well, now you drive me everywhere. I want to get my license, get a car, and be able to drive where I want to go."

"OK. We will need to talk about grades, how we will pay for the car, and a driving agreement."

"Sure. I suppose I will have to get a job to help with the insurance."

"That would be helpful. Also, we want to talk about you purchasing your own clothes, selecting a college, curfews, chores around the house, etc."

"Chores? What does that have to do with freedom? That's slavery!"

"If you want more freedom, you gotta have more responsibility. Plus, it will prepare you for your own place. For instance, this year you learn to cook; next year, when you have your license, you learn to shop. You see what I am saying?"

"So this is a countdown to my independence?"

"Yeah."

"I like that!"

"Me too. You might say it is my strategy to work myself out of a job. It is my 'De-parenting Plan.'"

"I'm still your child, aren't I?"

"Yes, and in three short years you will be empowered to take on life."

"Cool!"

SETTING A TARGET

What is your target? And I don't mean your teenager. I mean, "What is your goal in parenting your teenager?" If you don't have a parenting goal, how will you determine if you are parenting effectively? How will you know if you hit the target (or missed) if you don't have one?

If you need a goal, consider this idea from family counselor and best-selling author Norm Wright: "Our goal as parents is to empower our children to become mature and to release them to become independent from us and dependent on God."[2]

I like that, don't you? I think it captures the principle of progressive release; but it is reassuring to consider God's role. We don't have to parent alone. When we can't be with our kids, we can take comfort that they are not alone.

I like to tell parents, "If you are a believer and your teenager is too, the same Holy Spirit that is in you is in them. The Holy Spirit corrects, convicts, guides, comforts, and leads us in truth. Find release and encouragement in that promise." The challenge is to protect while we release.

As we empower our teenage children, we are affirming the "child's ability to learn, grow and become all that one is meant to be as part of God's image and creative plan."[3] Our partnership with the Creator is to help our teens learn and discover their full potential as His custom-made masterpieces.

TRUSTING YOUR TEEN

One night I had to trust our daughter. She said she was going to the mall with a friend to see a movie. I found out later that the movie was not playing at the theater in the mall. She was at the mall for three hours, not doing what I thought she would be doing for two of those three hours. *Was she up to something? Did she meet another group of friends and do something different from what she told me? What was she really up to?* Those thoughts sprinted through my head. Fortunately, I had just written this chapter and soon recognized in my thinking some of the Barriers to Empowerment.

Our daughter has been responsible when we have let her go to the mall. She is trustworthy. *She probably read the movie section wrong; I have no reason to not trust her,* I began to reason.

We can't empower teens we don't trust. Trust is absolutely critical to releasing our teens and helping them toward independence. When teens complain that "No one trusts me!" there may be more behind the complaint. William L. Coleman suggests that teens need to feel trusted.

> When a daughter asks, "Do you trust me?" she would like to hear, "Yes, most of the time, but not always."
> In that statement she hears that she is generally trustworthy. She hears encouragement, but not foolhardy release. She can then build on the affirmation that her parent trusts her.
> If we say we don't trust them at all, we destroy their confidence; but if we say we trust them entirely, we place too much burden on their shoulders.[4]

Your teen also wants to see that trust grow, Coleman notes.

> What could be more frustrating for a teenager who always gets good grades than to hear his parents ask every

evening, "Do you have your homework done?" The evidence that he handles his academic work well should create trust. *When a teenager feels as if he can never please his parents, he will become angry, frustrated, and develop a shaky sense of worth.*

Likewise, steady, dependable performance should result in added trust. If your teenager never gets into trouble, don't tell him every time he goes out not to get into trouble. What's the point of hassling the kid?[5]

Trust needs to be earned, but sometimes it needs to be given. It's true in all relationships. Sometimes we have to rebuild the trust.

SEVEN TIPS FOR MOTIVATING YOUR TEEN

Empowerment involves helping our teens internalize values and encouraging them toward independence. The whole process requires energy. In case you haven't noticed, being a parent of a teenager can be very exhausting. It is difficult to have energy to bring to the parenting table. Sometimes it is difficult to get *ourselves* motivated, let alone our teenagers!

Here are my humble tips for motivating your teen.[6] They may not always work, but if you find something that always works with teens let me know, and I'll put it in my next book and give you credit and a free copy.

1. Allow Your Teen to Fail.

Some of life's lessons can be learned only in failure. Allow your teen to learn from his mistakes. Rescuing him may make him more comfortable, but it is also likely to make him more foolish. A wise person embraces the lessons he can learn from failure.

Don't try to keep your teen from all failure. Don't rush in and always rescue him. When a teen fails, he begins to understand the limits of his strengths and the inevitability of his weaknesses. Failure forces him to develop a realistic self-appraisal and to accept responsibility.

I like that saying, "No one is a failure until they blame someone else."

2. Limit What You Give to Your Teenager.

We may give in to our teens because we are afraid of their rejection or their negative behavior. If we are going to motivate them, we have to be firm. We have to set boundaries. We have to be willing to say no and stick to it.

They may whine and go on about what they "need," but your job is to provide them with their genuine needs, not their wants. Like us, our teens need only a few essential things. When we limit what we give, we are modeling self-restraint.

Saying "no" teaches another important lesson to teens. It teaches them to wait. That's important when instant gratification is the longing of youth. As popular youth speaker and author Ken Davis notes, "Slavery to immediate gratification is the basis of many of the destructive experiences of adolescence and early adulthood, such as experimentation with drugs, premarital sex, and the bondage of debt."[7]

3. Teach and Model Respect for People and Property.

Do your kids appreciate what they already own? Do they care for their stuff and show respect for the property of others? One of our jobs is to train our teens to care for people and care for their property. This helps them learn value. If they understand the worth of something, they might treat it better. If teens understand this, they won't steal or destroy. Graffiti is an example of a lack of respect for others and their property.

People who are respectful are motivated and motivating. A lack of respect breeds a lack of motivation. Your teenager needs to learn respect by watching you.

Your teen is watching. Is he learning how to respect others by watching you?

Think of ways your teen can show respect for people. For instance, we have tried to encourage our teenage daughters to write thank-you notes for gifts they receive. We also have instructed Nicole and Brooke to use manners. I am amazed at the lack of social grooming done by parents, as evidenced by a lack of manners with some teens. Your own teen can learn to model respect for people and property as you model and give him or her opportunities to practice good behaviors.

4. Build into Your Teen the Value of Completion.

Teens have many more options. than we had at their age. Besides the music lessons and the conventional high school sports of our day, now boys can play soccer and water polo, and girls can play basketball and volleyball at their schools. To help motivate our teens, we need to help them complete what they begin. They gain a sense of achievement and closure when we complete a project, when we finish an athletic season, and when we complete a series of lessons.

How do we help our teens complete what they start? Answer: "Start fewer things." Some teens are too busy with too many activities. Maybe they would bring more motivation to an activity if it were the only thing they were doing besides school. Teach them be selective with their activities.

5. Limit Exposure to Media.

Our teenagers are prone to media mania. Watching TV, surfing the Internet, listening to FM radio, playing video games, and gazing at videos can lead to information overload. Their brains are filled with useless information. Maybe that is why they have a difficult time studying for tests!?

The bombardment of data requires processing. Processing demands time and mental focus. It can't be rushed. Have you noticed that when your teen is overstimulated she becomes apathetic and passive?

Increase your teen's motivation; create time for her to process data, to wrestle with big thoughts, to daydream, to discover new ideas, and maybe even *read a book.*

6. Work Together.

Some parents try motivating their teens by bribing them. This can work for the short-term, but it doesn't develop internal motivation. Instead, design a project that benefits someone else. Serve soup to the homeless. Go on a short-term mission trip together. Research community needs and partner with other families with teens to meet a need. Relationships grow deep in service.

A completed project helps you to connect with your teen. It motivates your teen. And it makes your teen feel competent and capable.

7. Play Together.

A lot of parents I know who are working hard on their relationship with their teen would be better off if they worked less and played harder. I learned this principle as a youth pastor. I played a lot with the students in my youth group. We played sports, water skied, surfed, snow skied, went to concerts, had car rallies, played hide-and-seek, and went on bike tours and backpack trips. You can really connect with a teen when you are playing together.

Teens have confided in me that their parents aren't any fun. They don't open up with their parents or want to spend time with them because they are too serious. I could tell you dozens of stories of how teens have opened their hearts to me about things they have never shared with their parents. Each story involves playing first, then relaxing for a few minutes afterward.

Try it and see if it builds motivation and connection with your teen. When we play and laugh with our teens, we build a bond with them. Play creates a sense of belonging. It makes one feel whole. Having fun together can motivate us.

For "Almost Cool" Parents

1. Mention the top two values from the family values exercise (page 128). What is the most important value that you want to pass on to your teen?

2. Tell the group the idea you put into the "new idea column." (If you have not done this exercise, complete it this week at home.)

3. Which of the fifteen "Things to Do" would you like to practice to encourage your teen? Which of the fifteen "Things to Say" do you think would make a positive impact on your teen?

4. Review the four barriers to empowering your teen. Try to give an example of each.

5. What has worked to motivate your teen?

Chapter 9
DEALING WITH
AN ANGRY TEEN

Having teenagers in the house can be irritating. I know that may be an insight into the obvious, but it felt good to write it. It felt honest. Pretending our teens don't ever bother us isn't healthy. It's OK to admit that our teens make us angry at times. We know they get angry at us.

How are we supposed to deal with anger in the parent-teen relationship?

Solution #1: Send them to boarding school.

OK, so that isn't reasonable for you. What else can you do when anger is breaking the peace and quiet of your domicile?

Learn your three R's.

I'll explain. Once upon a time there was a youth pastor (me) who wanted to help the nice parents of the teens in his youth group. He started a Parents' Discussion Group to talk about raising teenagers. After several weeks of meeting, one of the mothers shared her experience with her daughter's rebellion:

"It took us years to get through it. It was horrendous. I realize now that I was contributing to my daughter's rebellion."

The parents in the circle leaned forward to listen.

"I have discovered a principle that has revolutionized our relationship: *Rules without Relationship lead to Rebellion*. I was real good at forcing the rules on her, but not as good at developing a relationship with her. I contributed to her rebellion. Remember these three R's if you have teenagers."

RULES AND REBELLION

I like what she said: "Rules without relationship lead to rebellion." The three R's in action. But not everyone agreed with her. Mr. White came up to me privately after the meeting to challenge the statement.

"Tim, I gotta tell you. I didn't like what that woman said. My kids aren't going to rebel. I am the authority, and they will do what I say."

Being a young father, I wanted to learn from his pronouncement. I took out my notepad and jotted some of his phrases.

"It's my way or the highway. My rules, my house; love it or leave it. Teens need a firm hand to keep them from rebelling," said Mr. White. He seemed a little perturbed.

"Thanks for sharing with me. I have only been a father for a short while. I'll be interested to see what works." I wasn't sure about his approach.

Mr. White's Rebel Daughter

It didn't take long for me to notice the results of his approach. Mr. White had two teenage daughters in the youth group. Dianne was the older one. At fourteen, she was an enthusiastic and outgoing teenager. But during her sophomore year she began to change. The first thing I noticed was her eye makeup. It was heavy and dark. The second thing I noticed was her frown. She no longer looked happy. She looked mad. Even her makeup looked like it was applied to project rage.

She was forced to come to youth group by her father. She really wasn't a problem once she got there; but I could tell she made a big battle about it every week. She was doing what most teenagers do when they get mad. They push their parents' buttons. She knew church was important to her dad, so she acted like it was offensive to her and a complete waste of time. At least in front of him.

This went on for a year. One afternoon during her junior year, she stopped by unexpectedly to see me.

"I need to talk with you for a minute. I'm sorry."

"Come on in, Dianne. I'm glad to see you. What's up?" I then noticed her bloodshot eyes. I wondered if she had been drinking or smoking marijuana.

"I'm in big trouble."

Thinking it was substance abuse, I made an open-ended comment: "Yeah, you look like something is going on."

"He's going to kill me!" she exclaimed, and then started sobbing.

I reached for the tissues. "Here, have a tissue. Who is going to kill you?"

"I can't believe this is happening to *me!*"

"Is Louie going to kill you?" I asked about her boyfriend, commonly referred to in the youth group as "Scuzzy Louie." He was one of the greasiest lowlifes in town.

"No, not Louie. My *dad* is going to kill me!"

My eyes dropped from looking at her blotchy face to her stomach. "You're pregnant?" I asked softly, hoping my hunch was wrong.

"Yeah. I've tested twice. I'm definitely pregnant."

All of the sudden I became afraid. Not for Dianne and this unplanned pregnancy, but for myself. I felt the anxiety of the impending rage of Mr. White. He was a big and angry man. I was scared.

"You have to go with me to tell him."

Her words jarred me. "What?!"

"You have to go with me to tell my dad, so he won't kill me."

"But he might kill me!" I was dead serious. Mr. White

belonged to the National Rifle Association and had a huge gun cabinet. I'd been to their house. I'd seen his deer rifle, his rabbit rifle, his pistols, and his anger. It was a frightening moment.

"You have to, you're my youth pastor!"

At that moment I wanted to be anything but her youth pastor. A garbage collector, a sewer worker, a complaint window clerk, or even a junior high substitute teacher—I would gladly have been anything but a youth pastor.

I heard myself say, "Let's pray." *Should I pray?* Afterward, I told my administrative assistant, "If I'm not back by 5:30, call 911." I was only half-kidding.

I drove to their house with fear and trembling. The twenty-minute drive seemed like hours. Mr. White met us in the living room. I sat on the couch, about three feet away from Dianne. I didn't want to sit too close to her when she sprang the news. I didn't want Hair-trigger to think I was the father!

Mr. White stood in front of the fireplace. He had just stoked the fire. Placing the black, iron tool in the holder, he stood up straight, fixed his eyes on me, and demanded, "What's going on?"

It was then that I noticed two things: how tall he really was, and the gun cabinet to his immediate left. I was calculating how many seconds I would have if he went for the rifle, when I heard Dianne say, "Dad, I'm sorry to tell you. I know you will be mad, but I'm pregnant."

I was shocked at the strength in her voice.

Instantly, Mr. White fixed his eyes on me.

"No, Dad, it's not Tim. He's here for my support. It's with Louie." She burst into uncontrollable sobbing.

Mr. White's Reaction

Mr. White made a quick move. Startled, I retreated back into the safety of the couch. But he didn't go left toward the gun cabinet. He went right, around the coffee table and directly to Dianne. He scooped her up in his arms and cra-

144

dled her. When she felt his embrace, she released her emotions even more. She began to wail.

After five or ten minutes of crying and embracing, I heard him say, "Dianne, will you forgive me? I was too harsh and didn't take the time to know you or understand you."

"Sure, Daddy, I forgive you. Do you forgive me?"

"Yes, Dianne, I forgive you. Don't worry, we'll get through this together."

Her face lit up like a neon light. She was expecting rejection and anger. She received forgiveness and grace. She leaned her damp cheek against his chest. Stroking her hair with his right hand, embracing her with his left, he repeated, "We'll get through this together. Don't you worry. I love you."

She stiffened as if she was stung by a cattle prod on her back side. She pulled back, far enough to stare into his eyes. Then she pulled herself in close to him. She told me later, "I was stunned. That was the first time I can remember my dad telling me that he loved me."

I sat on the couch dumbfounded. I had just observed a miracle. We had prayed for a change of heart for Mr. White; but when you see it happen in front of your eyes, it is still unbelievable!

We talked for a while about what Dianne could do. When it came time for me to leave, Mr. White asked, "Tim, remember in the parents' class a woman said 'Rules without relationships leads to rebellion'?"

"Yeah, I remember."

"It's really true. I wish I had listened two years ago. Maybe this could have been avoided. Thanks for that class, and for your support today."

I was speechless. Something like that doesn't occur too often to me. I mumbled, "You're welcome, glad to help."

Months later, Dianne gave birth to a beautiful baby and gave her up for adoption. Through the whole process her father was supportive and attentive. It revolutionized their relationship. Dianne dumped Scuzzy Louie, finished high school, and went off to college. She met a handsome, Christian man; they fell in love and were married.

At a recent wedding, I saw Dianne with her young son and the proud grandfather, Mr. White. "We've learned a lot about kids and grandkids," he said grinning.

"Like rules without relationship lead to rebellion," added Dianne, smiling back at her father.

ANGER IS NOT ILLEGAL

Many of us grew up in homes where anger was considered illegal. The expression of anger was a sign of rebellion. In some families, this is still true. Anger was always under the surface in the White home; but it was never dealt with until Dianne became pregnant. Unexpressed anger can be very dangerous. Youth expert Ken Davis warns: "Since teens and preteens spend a good part of their life feeling angry, you must allow for the expression of anger if you want your kid to talk to you at all."[1]

Our Angry Teens

Our teens are going to be angry. We are going to be angry. We need to find ways to express anger that won't be destructive or hidden. Anger isn't a sin, whether it's displayed by you or your child. It is a God-given emotion that acts as a warning light that something is wrong. It prepares us to take action. Consider the biblical view of anger in two New Testament verses:

"In your anger do not sin" (Ephesians 4:26).

"Everyone should be quick to listen, slow to speak and *slow to become angry*" James 1:19 (italics added).

Note that the apostle James didn't write, "Everyone shouldn't be angry." Instead, the warning is about getting hotheaded and expressing anger in a reactive or defensive manner.

Anger, directed at the right source, at the right time, in the right way, is appropriate. Jesus expressed appropriate anger on several occasions.

With teenagers, the danger is that they will not express the anger they feel. Ross Campbell, a doctor of pediatrics and associate professor at University of Tennessee College of Medicine, describes the passive-aggressive response common to many teens when they have anger:

> Passive-aggressive behavior is the opposite of an open, honest, direct, and verbal expression of anger. Passive-aggressive behavior is an expression of anger that gets back at a person indirectly. A few examples of this are procrastination, dawdling, stubbornness, intentional inefficiency, and "forgetfulness." The subconscious purpose of passive-aggressive behavior is to upset the parents or parent-figures and to make them angry. Passive-aggressive techniques of handling anger are indirect, cunning, self-defeating, and destructive. Unfortunately, passive-aggressive behavior is subconsciously motivated; that is, the child is not consciously aware that he is using this resistant, obstructive behavior to release his pent-up anger to upset his parents.[2]

Some parents of teens are so frustrated with this behavior that they really clamp down, only to discover that their teen continues to misbehave. The teens' motive is to upset their parents. Yet, as Dr. Campbell notes, the teens often are not even aware of this drive within themselves.

The challenge is to find some appropriate expression of anger. If you don't permit your teens to discover a healthy way to express their anger, it will smolder and grow and find its expression in another, less acceptable way.

Four Things that Provoke Teens

Teens get angry. What are some things that we do to annoy them? Four behaviors by parents can create frustration and anger for teens.[3]

1. *Put-downs and sarcasm.* Even if meant in fun, these kinds of comments are taken as statements of personal disap-

proval. You may mean, "I don't like those pants," but your teen hears, "I don't like you."

2. *Expecting her to act like an adult because she looks like one.* Teens may have a mature body, but their emotions and thinking may take some time to catch up. Expecting teens to live up to adult expectations creates frustration.

3. *Assuming that what worked before will work now.* Just when we figure out how to parent our ten year old, he changes, and a whole new set of parenting tools is required. The old stuff simply does not work! Have you noticed "Because I said so" doesn't work as well as it used to?

4. *Minimizing feelings.* A breakup with a boyfriend is a huge event for your daughter. She may feel loss, rejection, confusion, anger, or a combination of these. Comments like, "You'll find another boyfriend soon," or "There are plenty of fish in the sea," hurt. They communicate to her that you are not taking her feelings seriously. You may be right, but the pain she feels at that moment is what is important.

DEALING WITH CONFLICT AND ARGUMENTS

Some parents and teens are discouraged and disillusioned when it comes to their parent-teen relationship. Often the reason for this is the inability to deal with conflict. One reason conflict happens is because parents have difficulty perceiving their teen's needs.

Teens say, "I want to be treated like an adult with trust and respect."

The Challenge of Conflict

Parents have the challenge of dealing with conflict without overcorrecting or exasperating their kids. When teens are asked what their parents do to make them mad, most teens respond: "They talk too much and too long about the same old thing."

To discover what "old record" you might be playing, try this exercise. On a sheet of paper list the "Top Ten Conflict Areas." Make number one the area that causes the most conflict with your teen; number ten the least. Ask your teen to privately develop his own Top Ten list; then compare lists. See if you agree on common conflict areas. Negotiate a new, rewritten list that you both can support for the top five conflict areas.

You haven't solved any of the conflicts, you have simply identified them.

The best way to deal with conflict is to talk with your teen ahead of time about how to argue or disagree. This will help you grow together and learn from conflict, rather than create distance in your relationship.

The Arguments of Teens

Parents who never discuss hot issues with their teens risk causing them to hold in their emotions. This approach causes some teens to become bitter, resulting in no dialogue

---

Chart 7
WHEN CONFLICT COMES

Parents who care are parents who are involved, and this will mean conflict at times. When your teen and you disagree, don't forget the rules for disagreeing discussed in this chapter (pages 151–53):

Do	Don't
1. Listen carefully	1. Overreact
2. Use the Golden Rule	2. Jump to conclusions
3. Define and discuss the conflict	3. Be hurtful
4. Recognize your contribution to the problem	
5. Discuss possible solutions	
6. Decide on a solution	
7. Evaluate the solution	

---

at all. Their inability to discuss issues, even debate, can cause teens to give up and hide their feelings. Others will become argumentative, trying to one-up the parent while avoiding a dialogue. As William L. Coleman notes:

> Teenagers can be quite clever and convincing when it comes to arguing a point. No longer in a mode to only please their parents, they are getting good at finding loopholes in their parent's logic. This is a major step in their separation ritual. They have begun to think on a similar plane as adults. . . . Debating with a teenager can be exhausting. They are smart, quick, great observers, have terrific memories (when they want to remember), and they gather techniques from their friends and siblings. Young people come to court with a well-stocked arsenal.
>
> On the other hand, parents often arrive empty-handed. They may even think an argument shouldn't happen because
>
> • They think the teen should simply obey.
> • They think there should be no negotiation.
> • They are certain they know best.
> • They refuse to be flexible as the youth grows older.
> • They confuse the important with the peripheral.
>
> Not all parents think this way, or are totally unprepared for confrontation. Some handle discussion or argument smoothly. But many of us learn the way it should have been done only after our teenagers have grown and left home.[4]

Often the parent should respond with firmness, Coleman adds. "If the situation should not be compromised, then don't compromise. Firmness at the right time provides security. Be willing to listen, but don't confuse the orange with the peel."[5]

With teenagers in the home, everyday may look like *People's Court!* Arguing is a basic need for teens. When we spend time debating our teens, we demonstrate respect by taking the time and focus to intellectually spar with them. This is helpful to the development of their logic and reasoning abilities. It also helps them feel that their viewpoint is valid enough to discuss. A teenager reasons, *If they value my opinion enough to debate it, they must value me enough to try to understand me.*

HOW TO "FIGHT FAIR"

Of course, when debating our teens we have to be careful; they know how to push our buttons and get us to react. Let me offer you some ideas on arguing with your teenager.

What Not to Do

Here are some warnings as you enter into disagreement with your teen, some rules of engagement.

1. *Don't overreact.* Scripture warns us to be "quick to listen, slow to speak and slow to become angry" (James 1:19). Sometimes we quickly get sucked into the intensity of the argument and explode. We imagine the worst-case scenario and allow our emotions and fears to affect our response to a conflict.

2. *Don't jump to conclusions.* I think some parents' only exercise is jumping to conclusions. It takes time, patience, and research to really understand a situation. That's why Proverbs 29:20 warns: "Do you see a man who speaks in haste? There is more hope for a fool than for him."

3. *Don't be hurtful.* Don't shame your teenager by degrading him or her. Focus on his wrong behavior, not on him as a person. Never get physical or threaten to hurt him. This doesn't resolve conflict; it generally makes it worse.

What to Do

Here are some suggestions on holding a fair argument with your teen, on how to "fight fair."

1. *Listen carefully.* It is crucial that parents and teens really try to hear what each other is saying. It is important to choose a time to deal with a conflict which allows both par-

ties to listen without being distracted and to approach conflict with an attitude of humility and patience.

2. *Use the Golden Rule.* Jesus commanded that we treat others as we wish to be treated: "Do to others as you would have them do to you (Luke 6:31). Often called the "Golden Rule," this is a very useful parenting principle. Ask yourself, *How would I want to be treated if the situation were reversed and I was the teenager?*

Sometimes we can gain perspective by switching roles and imagining the other person's point of view and feelings.

3. *Define and discuss the conflict.* Take time to describe the problem specifically and objectively. Let each party share his or her perspective. Seek first to understand, rather than be understood. As Paul has written, "Do nothing out of selfish ambition or vain conceit, but in humility consider others better than yourselves. Each of you should look not only to your own interests, but also to the interests of others" (Philippians 2:3–4).

4. *Identify and accept your contribution to the problem.* Be willing to admit your mistakes and ask forgiveness where called for. Making yourselves vulnerable to each other will help in resolving the conflict and strengthening your relationship.

Teens are looking to see if we will be authentic and responsible. If we contribute to the conflict but don't own up to it, they will write us off as phony. In some cases, I believe teens instigate a conflict with us just to see how we will handle it. They want to see if we will take responsibility for our own behavior. If they push our buttons, and we overreact, they are waiting to see if we own that behavior, or try to blame it all on them.

Being real with each other, forgiving each other, and praying together will restore a broken parent-teen relationship. It is God's recipe for healing. That's why the apostle James wrote, "Confess your sins to each other and pray for each other so that you may be healed" (James 5:16).

5. *Discuss possible solutions.* Help your teens develop healthy conflict resolution skills. I believe God designed parent-teen conflict as a means of teaching teens these skills, and to prepare them for larger conflicts that they will encounter later in life.

6. *Decide on a possible solution.* What steps are necessary for a change? Do we need to compromise? If both parent and teen are involved in choosing the possible solution, it increases the likelihood of avoiding future conflict over the issue. Conflict can lead to unity if we take the time to work toward a mutually acceptable solution.

7. *Evaluate the solution.* After the solution has been implemented, evaluate to see if it is working. Ask your teen for his evaluation. If he doesn't feel that the conflict has been resolved, be willing to take another look at it. Don't assume that you will get it right with the first attempt.

Christians have conflict. Just because we have Christ in our lives doesn't mean that we won't have conflict. There was conflict in the early church. Scripture teaches us how that conflict was resolved (Acts 15). According to church history, to resolve the disagreement, they called a council. In other words, they discussed the issues. They showed value to their opponents by talking about the conflict. They didn't sweep it under the carpet or ignore it, hoping it would go away. Reconciliation requires discussion. When we don't talk about conflict, we demean our teens. In a way, we *cancel* them. We dismiss their opinion and worth.

Instead of "canceling" them, let's set up a council. Discuss the issue with your teen. When it comes to conflict, you have a choice: *cancel* or *counsel*.

WHEN TEENS FEEL HOSTILE AND HOPELESS

Teens are angry. Many of them are angry at their parents. "Thanks for nothing!" is the slogan of angry youth. Much of this anger comes from kids who felt that their parents weren't there when they needed them. Richard Louv, in his book *Childhood's Future,* discusses this: "To whom do children turn when their parents do not have enough time for them? To other time givers, some benign, some not so benign. To peers, to gangs, to early sex partners, to the new electronic bubble of computers and video."[6]

With divorce, Mom and Dad at work, and the pinch of economics, kids have less and less time with their parents. What used to be restricted to urban areas has now become a suburban problem. The networks that used to protect children have fallen apart. There is a great loss of connectedness in our culture. As we have less positive family time, we increase the sense of being disconnected and vulnerable. Gangs have become surrogate parents for some teens.

Teens who join gangs often feel disconnected from their families. The gang gives them a place to belong and an opportunity to vent. When our teens feel hostile and hopeless, they become self-destructive or aggressive. Our goal is to help them learn appropriate ways to process their anger. This gives them a sense of control. They may not be able to control many aspects of their lives; but if they can control themselves, it gives them hope.

DEALING WITH ANGER

Several years ago, I invited psychologist and author Dennis Guernsey to speak to our youth group. He taught a very practical lesson on anger. I have since used it in my own life and in my counseling and teaching.

"How many of you get angry?" Dr. Guernsey asked a packed room of high school students. They all raised their hands, except for the ones in the back; they weren't quite awake yet.

Anger and a Chicken

"When you get angry, I want you to think of a chicken."
Grumbles and stares from the teenage crowd.

"That's right, a chicken. Next time you get angry, think of a chicken. Can you all picture a chicken? Try it right now. OK, got it? Actually, I want you to think of a hen. But most of us do anyway. Remember that, because it will really be useful the next time we get angry. Who makes you mad?"

"My parents," said one.

"My pesky little brother," snickered another

"My wicked stepmother."

"My biology teacher. He's annoying."

"Great," said Dr. Guernsey. "So you all have someone that makes you mad. Now think of that person. Now think of a hen clucking around that person. Got it?"

The students looked somewhat bewildered, but they still listened closely.

"When you get angry, try this experiment. It might help you deal with your anger. Remember the formula: A HEN. *A* stands for *anger*. Next time you are angry, say to yourself, *I believe I am angry*. The first key to controlling your anger is acknowledging that you get angry. Next, say to yourself, *I am angry because I am* H—hurt. Most of the time we are angry because someone hurt us in some way. Identifying the hurt can help us not immediately retaliate.

"Next, say to yourself, *I am* hurt *because of* E—expectations. *I had expectations that weren't met.*

"When we begin to think of the expectations we had, it helps us process our anger," Guernsey explained. "We can ask ourselves if we had realistic expectations or not. We can ask, *Have I communicated my expectations?* Many times people get angry over uncommunicated expectations. We assumed that the other person would magically understand what we wanted. Are you still with me?"

The students were listening; some were taking notes. Even the guys in the back row had woken up and were paying attention. There is something about the topic of anger that touches each of our hearts.

Anger and Our Needs

"Now this is an important part. The last letter in our A HEN formula is the letter N. That stands for our *needs*. When you get angry it usually is because you were hurt because your expectations were not met. Now here is the tricky part. Ask yourself: Were those expectations based on needs or wants? If your needs were not met, you have a right to be angry. But if your expectations were based on wants you may not have a right to be angry. Anger is the surface signal. Take time to find out the root cause, then you will know what to do with it."

A girl in the front raised her hand. "Can you give me an example of needs versus wants?" she asked.

"Sure. Let's say it is a hot day and you are walking home from school. You imagine getting home and having a big bowl of your favorite ice cream. You can picture the chocolate chip cookie dough as you walk and sweat. You get home and discover that your little brother has beaten you to the ice cream and eaten all of it. You are angry. Is this based on an expectation of need or want?"

"Want, I guess."

"You're right. You don't need ice cream to survive, but it helps. But now think about needs. If you went to the pantry and discovered no food of any kind, that would be a genuine need not being met. We must eat. That is a basic need. Understanding what makes us angry is half the battle in figuring out what to do with it."

A HEN: anger, hurt, expectation, and need. This is a tool to help process anger. As a parent, you can use it with yourself and with your teenager. I have found that it is much more helpful to discuss with teens their expectations and needs rather than anger and hurt. We can usually do something about meeting a person's needs or expectations. But it is much more difficult to resolve conflict if we stay focused on anger and hurt.

LEVELS OF ANGER

Anger isn't all at one level.[7] Some anger is stealth vengeance. Other anger is violent and visible. Some anger is directed at the source and other anger isn't. Our goal as parents of teenagers is twofold: (1) to model appropriate ways to process anger, and (2) to help our teens move from inappropriate to appropriate ways to express anger.

Level one anger is *passive-aggressive behavior.* Forgetting to do chores, not taking care of property, teasing, being obnoxious or loud, and not doing well at school are all common ways teens express anger. They may not realize they are angry. These behaviors may not be intentional, but they are revealing. At other times, passive-aggressive behavior is intentional. That is when our teens *push our buttons!*

Level two anger is *negative behavior.* Throwing objects, swearing, displacing anger, complaining, and threatening are common behaviors at this level. These are easier to deal with because they are identifiable. Passive-aggressive behavior is covert and slippery to deal with.

Level three anger is *positive and negative behavior.* It includes focusing anger on the source, sticking to the main complaint, thinking logically, and being passionate but in control. At this level, parents and teens can begin working through the A HEN process and work toward understanding the issues.

Level four anger is *process-focused.* The anger is focused on the source, but the goal is resolution (not revenge). Side issues are not brought into the discussion, even though there is hurt and pain. At this level listening and reason are critical parts of the discussion. This is the level we want to be with our teenagers when we, or they, are angry. At this level, we can work toward reconciliation. We can process our anger because we feel safe. No cheap shots taken.

Our aim is to encourage our teens to move up the anger levels, even if it is one level at a time. Try applying these with your teenager. Define and contrast the different levels with her/him. Discuss how a discussion on expectations and needs is more helpful than one on hurt and anger. I have noticed that people are much more responsive when you discuss needs, not demands.

For example, you can say, "I am angry because I feel hurt. You didn't clean up the living room like you promised. I was expecting you to. I was at work all day and needed you to do your part. My need was for you to help us get ready for company. I feel you were not considerate to my need."

This type of conversation can help a parent express her anger, model the A HEN process, and also hold her teen accountable for his behavior.

If you have teens, they will anger you. It's a law of science. The wise parent has developed a way to process her anger, and to help her teen process his.

For "Almost Cool" Parents

1. In their dramatic meeting at Dianne's home, the author and Mr. White learned anew the principle "Rules without relationship lead to rebellion." What else did you learn from this story?
2. Review the "Four Things That Provoke Teens" (pages 147–48). Is there one that stands out because it points a finger toward you? What could you do to be less provoking to your teen?
3. Having teens in your house will lead to conflict. Does that bother you? Are you a peace-at-all-costs person, or can you mix it up a little and be confrontational?
4. "How to Fight Fair" gives nine ideas (beginning on page 151) on dealing with conflict in a healthy way. Give some examples of how *not* to deal with conflict. In other words, of "How to Fight Dirty." Do any of these look familiar?
5. How could you use the A HEN approach in a parent-teen conflict over curfew?

Chapter 10
DEALING WITH A HURTING TEEN

As a freshman in high school, I had mixed feelings. Anticipation, excitement, and pride combined with fear, intimidation, and embarrassment during my first day. One of the first things I noticed was how many cars were in the parking lot and how few bikes were in the rack. This place was different from junior high school!

As I wandered down the halls I noticed that the guys in the varsity jackets looked like men. The cheerleaders looked like cover girls. The teachers looked like war criminals in hiding. The school was run by administrators who dressed like Mister Rogers, even the women.

I survived my first morning, only to be haunted by the question, *Who will I eat lunch with?* I had not been able to find my friends. I ate alone that day, and several days afterward. The companionship of my Mountain Dew and Hostess cherry fruit pie didn't dull the pain of loneliness.

After ten lonely lunches (remember, I was a freshman) I discovered that a large group of kids ate across the street at Ricky's Burgers. I decided to check it out. The kids at the greasy drive-in didn't look like the students who ate in the cafeteria. They wore jeans and T-shirts; not slacks and button-down shirts.

I ordered a "Classic Burger, fries, and a Coke." I grabbed it and sat down at a picnic table, well-marked with initials of high school couples. The food was pretty good, in spite of the grease. I wiped my oily forehead and looked around. *Everyone here looks a little greasy. Is it my imagination, or does every guy here look like James Dean with zits?* As I pondered my anthropological observation, a tall guy came up to me. His jeans were torn. He wore boots, a T-shirt, and shoulder-length, brown hair.

Pulling his hair from his eyes, he asked, "Are you new here?"

"Uh . . . yeah. I'm a freshman." Then I felt embarrassed, *Why did I have to tell him that?*

"Yeah, I figured. I'm Craig." He held out his hand for the cool-guy handshake. As my hand touched his, I realized he was the first person who had offered a handshake or a word of welcome to me. I had been at school for two weeks. "Why not eat lunch with our gang every day at Ricky's. We sit over there." He motioned to a picnic table covered with smoking students.

"Yeah, sure. Thanks," I responded timidly.

Craig introduced me to the "Rowdies at Ricky's," as they liked to be called. He also introduced me to cruising, parties, and beer.

It was exciting at first, but after a while it became predictable. Boy gets car, picks up girl. They get beer, go to party, make out, get in fight, go home separately. Next week, boy gets new girl. . . .

"Craig, it all seems kind of silly. People are so fake. They are pretending to have a good time, but they don't really seem to be," I complained to Craig one day at Ricky's.

"Smith, you aren't enjoying the party because you are flying too low," he said, looking over his shoulder, then into my eyes. "What you need are some of these. Then you will be skyin'." He pulled a handful of pills from his jacket pocket: reds, whites, bennies, yellow jackets, and some pink and purple capsules. He held them out to me.

I stared at those drugs and considered my options. Everything I had heard about drugs was negative: *They will control you. You will become addicted. They can destroy your health. They might kill you.* All those thoughts raced through my head.

Then I thought, *Craig is my friend. He is the first person to show care to me. We have fun together. If he thinks it is OK, it must be; after all, he is a junior.*

"Not today," I heard myself say, "I have practice coming up and coach would kill me if I came loaded."

"Cool. You know I'm always here for you, man. Whenever you want 'em, I got 'em." He smiled as he put the pills back into his leather jacket.

That day, Craig and I started to drift apart. I learned that his friendship was conditional. If I wouldn't use drugs, he wouldn't hang around me. He was afraid I would "narc" on him. For all his coolness, Craig was really fearful and selfish. If you didn't play the game his way, he didn't want to play.

As a freshman I learned that people who use drugs act like they are into freedom, but they seldom are truly free.

DEALING WITH THEIR HURTS: DRUGS, ALCOHOL, AND PARTIES

Many teens, feeling alone, alienated, or unsure of themselves, look to various activities to try to deal with the pain or confusion. Drugs, alcohol, and parties are the most common ways teens cope.

Why Teens Use Drugs and Alcohol

I asked a group of teenagers, "Why do you think some teens use drugs and alcohol?"

They shared five reasons why they or their friends had become involved with substance abuse:

1. *Pressure.* Many teens experience peer pressure to drink or take drugs. Others face internal pressures and feel a sense of relief when they are loaded.
2. *Escape.* Many teens live pain-filled, stressed-out lives. They want a break. Problems at home, financial worries, adolescent anxieties and problems with friends cause many to seek escape in drugs and alcohol.
3. *Availability.* Teens tell me that drugs and alcohol are always around. "You can get it anytime, anywhere." Our teens are surrounded by a substance-abusing environment.
4. *Curiosity.* Most teens start drinking or using drugs because they are curious. They wonder what it would feel like to be drunk or on a marijuana high. They wonder if they would have more courage to talk to that "special someone" if they were buzzed.
5. *Emptiness.* Teens who are substance abusers often struggle with feelings of worthlessness and emptiness. Drugs and alcohol can make you forget pain and emptiness. They will work every time and make you feel better (for a while). But they don't take away the emptiness.

Pressure, escape, availability, curiosity, and emptiness are five reasons teens abuse substances. I arrange the five in this order intentionally, for the five together spell out what teens are looking for: PEACE.

Peace is contentment and satisfaction with life. Peace is the inner strength that helps us endure outer trials. Peace gives us fortitude to stand up to peer pressure. Without peace, our hearts are troubled and hurting.

As Jesus, the true peace-giver, declared: "Peace I leave with you; my peace I give you. I do not give to you as the world gives. Do not let your hearts be troubled and do not be afraid" (John 14:27). The world cannot give lasting peace. That's why Jesus says His peace is not "as the world gives."

Teens need peace; without it, they resort to filling the empti-
ness with something that works. They seek to numb the pain.
But it doesn't really work, not in the long run. Youth expert
Jim Burns writes:

> People use drugs and alcohol to make them feel good, but
> what they don't realize is that something else very important
> takes place when they use drugs and alcohol to replace their
> pain. *They stop learning how to cope with stress.* Drug and
> alcohol use is a false coping mechanism for dealing with
> stress. It makes you feel better temporarily, but it doesn't
> help relieve the long-term problems. You wake up the next
> morning with the same problems, sometimes intensified, and
> with the need to decide again on how to cope with the
> stress.[1]

Genuine peace is possible, but we need to pursue peace
God's way. The youth culture tells teens to "Party hearty!" as
a way to escape hurt and pain. God's way is different.

"Is It a Sin to Party?"

I am often asked by teenagers, "Is it a sin to party?"

"Depends on what goes on at the party," I usually
answer.

They frown at me. I reach for my Bible and say, "A
Christian is supposed to live differently from the crowd."
Sometimes I read 1 Peter 4:2–5:

> As a result, [a Christian] does not live the rest of his earthly
> life for evil human desires, but rather for the will of God. For
> you have spent enough time in the past doing what pagans
> choose to do—living in debauchery, lust, drunkenness, or-
> gies, carousing and detestable idolatry. They think it strange
> that you do not plunge with them into the same flood of dis-
> sipation, and they heap abuse on you. But they will have to
> give account to him who is ready to judge the living and the
> dead.

"A Christian spends his time differently," I tell them. "He has 'been there, done that' when it comes to the usual things that happen at parties. And if you don't do it, they 'heap abuse on you.'"

"Yeah, they do," responded one experienced teen.

"The word *dissipation* means *waste*. God doesn't want us wasting our time on things that don't last or don't build His kingdom. Those are a few reasons why you should avoid parties where kids are abusing alcohol and drugs."

Discuss with your teens the clear mandate of 1 Peter 4. Ask them where they see the "flood of dissipation" in their world. Teens who sometimes talk about someone who is "wasted" will get the picture.

HELPING OUR CHILDREN TO SAY NO TO DRUGS

It's not enough to say to our teens, "Just say no!" Even young adolescents face temptation. Author and youth ministry veteran Dave Veerman understands that: "Remember also that junior highers are *pressured and tempted:* to drink, to be sexually active, and to do a host of other things they know are wrong. The teachers and politicians may preach Just Say No, but the movies, musicians, disc jockeys, and videos all shout, *"Just say yes."*[2]

Going Beyond a Slogan

Clearly, a slogan isn't enough to help our teens resist the temptation of substance abuse. The parent-teen relationship is one of the most crucial determinants of whether a teenager will experiment with drugs. A teen who has a close and supportive relationship with his parent(s) and who feels positive about himself will be at low risk for substance abuse. Teens who are regularly involved in athletics or church youth groups are also at low risk.

Teens are also at low risk if their parents band together with other parents to establish agreements regarding alcohol and drugs. If parents agree that no party in their home will be unsupervised or have alcohol or drugs, then they have established parental peer pressure. This strategy destroys one of the favorite teen arguments: "But Susie's parents let her do it."

To compete with the pressure of the culture, media, and peers, parents need to create their own pressure. It is a form of pushing back. Working together with other parents, we can set boundaries and support each other in keeping them. Picture your teen as a balloon. The outside pressure that they feel is seeking to shape them by pressing in on them. Our job, as parents, is to build into them pressure from the inside, so that they can resist the external pressure.

To help our kids build internal strength to resist the damaging forces around them, we need to encourage them and empower them. It will require our investment of time, focus, and example. We can't let a slogan (Just Say No) do our work for us.

In my discussions with youth, I have detected that many of them find the Just Say No campaign to be insulting. Teenagers agree that they need to say no. What they resent is the approach. Among their comments:

"It treats us like we are in fifth grade."

"It's an easy answer for a very difficult problem."

"When I am told no, I just want to go out and do it."

"Trying to scare us doesn't work as well as talking with us without using the fear tactics."

"They tell us no, but they don't tell us *why*."

I agree with them. We will need more than a slogan and a national ad campaign to help our teens resist substance abuse. By itself, Just Say No is an overly simplistic attempt to solve a very complex problem. As parents, we should not relegate our work to the government or the schools. We need to be the primary teachers of our teens in the area of chemical dependency. What they might get at school could be supportive to what we teach and model. Our teens deserve more than just what they get at school to help them navigate past potentially life-threatening habits.

Physician Victor Strasburger summarizes the problem:

> It doesn't take a specialist in adolescent medicine to tell you the obvious: Not only do teenagers resent being told what to do, they may react by doing precisely the opposite. . . . The slogan is just that—a slogan. It does not teach teenagers *why* they should say no or give them the skills to know *how* they should say no. In short, it treats them like children, which is one of the biggest mistakes you can make in trying to deal effectively with teenagers.[3]

Tips on Talking to Your Teens about Drugs

Are you looking for some tips on how to effectively talk with your teen about substance abuse? Take another look at the complaints from teens about the Just Say No campaign (see page 165). If you were to change each of these into a positive trait, you would have some proven guidelines for what works with teens. Consider the following seven tips:

1. Treat teens like young adults (not children).
2. Engage in dialogue and be willing to wrestle with the issues (rather than repeating simplistic slogans).
3. Understand that sometimes teens like to be contrary. If you come on strong they will too. (This is the adolescent tendency to be contrary just to "tick you off.")
4. Discussion and explanation work better with teens than fear and threats.
5. The most powerful teaching method is example. Ask your teens to follow your modeling.
6. Teens are more apt to learn from life skills than from campaign slogans.
7. Training for resisting substance abuse needs to be age-appropriate.

Consider the age and maturity of your teen and use a developmental approach (not a one-size-fits-all method).

Getting Your Teens to Say No If You Said Yes

I'm often asked, "How do you get your teens to say no to drugs if you said yes when you were a teen?" Others ask, "How do you get your teens to say no to alcohol if you said yes when you were a teen?"

If you tried a drug, whatever the reason (some thought marijuana was harmless or fell to social or personal pressures), you still have a right to speak to your children about the dangers of drug use.

Some parents ask me, "Should we lie to our kids about our past involvement with drugs and alcohol?" I don't think lying solves anything. (It also violates God's clear command.) Tell them what they need to know when they need to know it. Not more and not sooner. You could say something like, "I tried using drugs and alcohol as a teen to numb my pain. It worked for a few short hours, but the pain was still there. Sometimes it only made it worse. I risked addiction or doing something really dangerous while under the influence. I now understand how risky it was, I didn't then. I'm asking you to learn from my mistakes, so you don't have to make them."

An approach like this is truthful, humble, and responsible; but it doesn't glamorize the use of drugs or alcohol. In fact, it makes it look stupid. This is our goal. This is one time when you want to look stupid in front of your teenager. We want them thinking when they walk away, *I'll never be dumb enough to try that stuff.*

I would be pleased to have my teenager think that.

We don't need to go into a lot of details about our experience with drugs and alcohol. Mention that you used them, but always attach a consequence or a regret when you mention them. Our goal is to build into their awareness the fact that substance abuse has consequences.

Say to your teen, "A wise person can learn from another person's mistakes. A growing person learns from his own mistakes. A fool makes mistakes, but never learns from them or how to avoid them. I want you to learn from my mistakes, so you will become wise."

IF YOU SUSPECT SUBSTANCE ABUSE

"My sixteen-year-old son is acting strange. I suspect he is experimenting with drugs. What should I do?" asked the concerned mom. The creases in her face and the gray dread in her eyes spoke volumes.

"It's hard to admit that possibility, isn't it?" I asked.

"I never thought it would happen to us."

"Why do you suspect something?"

"I found a bag of marijuana hidden in his room. He said it was a friend's who had left it there when he spent the night."

"Do you believe him?"

"I want to," she said with a hopeful frown.

"I wouldn't."

Her face dropped.

"Be suspicious. Experts say that when you catch someone for the first time it is more like their tenth or twentieth time using. Teens are very resourceful in hiding their drug use. If they get caught, it could mean they are getting sloppy. For you to catch him means his judgment is being affected by the drug. It could be worse than you think. Trust your intuition."

She looked devastated. I don't make a habit of ruining parents' days; but this mom needed a dose of reality. She sighed heavily.

"I thought something was going on when he brought home a terrible report card. Then, two weeks later, I found the pot. He quit the soccer team and dug up a new set of grungy friends. Whenever I talk to him about these changes he gets really defensive. Are these things that should concern me, or are they normal for a teenage boy?"

"They aren't normal to happen all at once. In fact, they are classic signs that your son is using pot."

My words hit her like a slap. She needed a few moments to consider what I had said. Slowly, deliberately, she responded, "What can I do? . . . uh . . . I'm sorry . . . Where have I gone wrong?"

"Let's focus on your son's behavior, not on yours. Focusing on 'should-haves' will only lead to shame. Talk to your son about your concerns. Expect him to be defensive. You may not actually be talking to your son, but to a marijuana-influenced brain. Focus on his behavior, not his argument or reasons. You might call the school and ask how he is doing. Don't mention drugs; just ask about his behavior. If he is using, usually a pattern emerges."

If you are like this mother, suspecting drug use, don't dismiss the evidence of changed behavior, changed physical appearance, and especially drugs in the house. Investigate such clues. Get input from trusted adults in his life. See if they have noticed a change in behavior or attitude. Here again, don't mention drugs.

If they confirm a pattern of changed behavior, get help. Develop a plan for intervention. Get a professional assessment. Consider having your teen tested for drugs by your doctor. And if there is a history of addiction in your family, let your teen know this; he could be playing with fire and not know it.

OUR DUTY TO PROTECT

Our Duty

In chapter 7 we discussed how to talk with our teens about love and sex. Talking with your kids about substance abuse is not easy, either. But this can be done, even if your teen is already using drugs or drinking regularly.

The key is for parents to take responsibility. This duty can't be delegated to the school, the church, the media, or anyone else. Only a parent has the influence to help a teen change.

I like the concept of drug-proofing your teen, described by Jim Burns and Stephen Arterburn in their helpful book *Drug-Proof Your Kids:*

We can drug-proof our kids and save them from the pressure to use drugs or take the steps to stop using them. The idea is comparable to weatherproofing a home. You cannot do away with the weather. The storms and floods will come. But the wise person has prepared his or her home to withstand the forces of nature and not be destroyed. Likewise, drugs are there. Alcohol is always available. But the drug-proof child will not be destroyed by them.[4]

Principles to Protect Our Teens

Winter storms chill our lives at times. The wise family prepares for the frigid season by building on a solid foundation and insulating each child with love, support, and guidance. There are no foolproof formulas. There are no warranties that your teen will be drug-free. There are, however, principles and practices that will help you build the kind of protection that will help increase your teen's resistance to drug and alcohol use. Chart 8 (page 171) points to four of these principles and procedures you have available as a Christian parent.

A Drug-Proof Plan

In *Drug-Proof Your Kids,* Burns and Arterburn offer a six-point plan to help parents protect their children from and lead their children away from drug use (including tobacco, which has been shown to be addictive). Here is a summary of most of their plan.[5]

1. *Education.* Parents must know what they are talking about when it comes to substance abuse. Information must be age-appropriate and creatively passed on to their children.

2. *Prevention.* Prevention involves rewards for responsible behavior and restrictions following irresponsible behavior. The goal is to help teens feel good about right decisions and immediately feel the consequences of poor choices. Part of the plan could be a contract (see the sample "Contract for Life," on page 173).

3. *Identification.* Parents should know the signs of tobacco, alcohol, or drug abuse. Parents should know how to

Chart 8
PRINCIPLES OF STRENGTH
IN PREVENTING SUBSTANCE ABUSE

The following principles can give you strength and direction to help your teen resist substance abuse.

1. *You aren't parenting alone.* As a Christian parent, you have the company of the Holy Spirit to guide, instruct, remind, and comfort you. He is always abiding with you. Learn to lean on His leading (Galatians 5:16–26).
2. *God uses families to accomplish His will.* The family is custom-designed by God. He wants to protect it and help it grow. God cares about families and offers parenting principles in Scripture. These will help you set a standard for protection and will offer guidance for instruction (Ephesians 6:1–4).
3. *Love, support, and common sense will help you develop a strategy to keep your teens drug-free.* Be willing to talk with your children about drugs before they are teens. Help them see that *they* can make their own decisions and strategies when it comes to escaping the pull of alcohol and drugs.
4. *Develop a drug-proof plan.* Such a plan is an organized strategy to deal with the pressures to use any harmful substance—alcohol, drugs, or tobacco. Consistently communicate the plan to your children.

evaluate their teen's behavior to determine if intervention is necessary.

4. *Intervention.* If a substance abuse problem is identified, intervention is the parental action that will quickly deal with the undesirable behavior by seeking to extinguish it.

5. *Treatment.* There are many levels and kinds of treatment. There is no substitute if it is needed. Parents need to know where to get help and how to use available resources.

6. *Supportive Follow-up.* The entire family is involved in preventing a relapse by working through the recovery process as a family.

A CONTRACT FOR LIVING

I was talking to a mother who was upset that her daughter had come home late and drunk.

"I didn't know what to do. I know there should be a consequence, but I couldn't think of one. So I sent her to bed and let her know we would deal with it in the morning. You know, Tim, that is a really helpful tactic: If you don't have a consequence, send her to her room until you can think of one. It gives you a chance to cool down and think of one. It also gives the teen a time to sweat, worry, and think. I like it!"

"I agree," I said. "Punishing in anger at 1:00 A.M. with a loaded teenager is sure to fail. Good call."

"I decided to use the contract that they use for the Students Against Driving Drunk. I got a copy from the high school and discussed it with my daughter. She knows now that she can call me at any time and I will come pick her up. No hassles. No punishment."

"I think that is a great approach. How is it working?"

"She has called me twice and hasn't drank since that night."

"I'd call that success," I affirmed.

She smiled and said, "I call it love."

That mother has found help in drawing up a contract, an agreement between a parent and a teen that holds the teen accountable and lets the teen know you the parent will be there to help.

The contract developed by Students Against Driving Drunk (SADD) appears on page 173. It's a great model that you may want to use to help your child avoid being in a car after drinking or in a car with someone who has become intoxicated. Consider adapting this sample for your use. Having a contract in advance of the situation helps you and your teen to know what to do.

Contract for Life:
A Foundation for Trust and Caring[6]

By agreeing to this contract, we recognize that SADD encourages all young people to adopt a **substance-free** life style. We view this contract as a means of opening the lines of communication about drinking, drug use and traffic safety to ensure the safety of all parties concerned. We understand that this contract does not serve as permission to drink, but rather, a promise to be safe.

Young Adult:

I acknowledge that the legal drinking age is 21 and have discussed with you and realize both the legal and physical risks of substance use, as well as driving under the influence. I agree to contact you if I ever find myself in a position where anyone's substance use impairs the possibility of my arriving home safely. I further pledge to maintain safe driving practices at all times, including wearing my safety belt every trip and encouraging others to do the same.

_____
Signature

Parent or Gurardian:

Upon discussing this contract with you, I agree to arrange for your safe transportation home, regardless of time or circumstances. I further vow to remain calm when dealing with your situation and discuss it with you at a time when we are *both* able to converse calmly about the matter.

I agree to seek safe, sober transportation home if I am ever in a situation where I have had too much to drink or a friend who is driving me has had too much to drink. Recognizing that safety belt usage is a vital defense against death and injury on the highway, I promise to wear my safety belt at all times and encourage others to do the same.

_____
Signature

_____
Date

Read the contract another time. Does this sound like something you can present to your teenager? If so, please do. It can reduce a lot of anxiety and stress. It might keep your teen from making a disastrous choice.

Consider developing a contract with your preteen as early as fifth grade. You can adapt the contract to make it age-appropriate. Definitely have a contract if your child is in middle school or high school. Our children are faced with drugs and alcohol at a much earlier age than we were. Let's help prevent substance abuse by being alert and prepared.

TWO DEADLY DRUGS: NICOTINE AND ALCOHOL

This chapter has focused primarily on drug abuse. I know that many of you might be thinking, *I don't have to worry about that. My kid will never use drugs. I can't imagine him using cocaine or marijuana or taking pills.*

That may be, but the two most important drugs you need to worry about are nicotine and alcohol. Cigarettes and alcohol pose the greatest danger to your children.

Smoking is the leading cause of preventable deaths in the United States. Each year approximately one million teenagers begin smoking—almost three thousand teenagers each day. All it takes to get hooked is completely smoking three cigarettes.[7]

Alcohol and cigarettes are gateway drugs to other drugs. Kids who smoke or drink are at a much higher risk to go on to other drugs. We shouldn't take their abuse casually.

Substance abuse is only one way teens deal with pain. I have chosen to focus on it in this chapter because it is so prevalent. Some other ways teens deal with hurt are eating disorders, pregnancy, and suicide. Many of the principles for intervention would apply to these problems as well.

The decisions our teens make will determine the kind of people they will become. If we can help them make wise choices now, chances are, they will end well.

The alternative is frightening.

Teenagers subconsciously believe that they are immortal. Death isn't real to them. They feel good; they are strong and fast; they can see well; the end of life seems far away. So kids smoke, drink, take drugs, drive under the influence of alcohol or drugs, and engage in many other risky behaviors, truly believing that nothing can happen to them. And many die.[8]

For "Almost Cool" Parents

1. Do you think drugs or alcohol tempt your teen? Why or why not?
2. What have you told your teen about drugs, alcohol, and tobacco?
3. Does a contract (like the SADD contract on page 173) seem like it would work in your family?
4. The five reasons that teens are substance abusers spell *peace*, but bring chaos: pressure, escape, availability, curiosity, and emptiness. Which of these five do you think your teen may be feeling now?
5. If you could give a one-sentence message about substance abuse to every teenager in the country, what would you say?

Chapter 11
HELPING TEENS
MAKE WISE DECISIONS

If only I could get her into Christian school, then she would be surrounded by positive peer pressure," said the mother of a fourteen year old as she dabbed at the tear in her eye.

I noticed the wrinkles around her eyes—too many for a woman her age. *She must worry a lot,* I thought. "Do you think being in a Christian school will help Liz?"

"She's just not good at making choices. She chooses the *worst* friends!" I noticed her eyebrows bend. She sounded angry.

"And you think by placing her in a Christian school she will learn how to make better choices?"

"Yes. She will have only good, solid, Christian kids to hang out with. The problem is the public schools."

I was worried about her perspective, but Linda was determined. The next semester Liz was enrolled at a Christian high school. She didn't want to leave her friends at the public high school; but her mom made her.

Within days of starting the new school, Liz found the one student with a similar defiant attitude. They quickly became friends. Linda was pleased that Liz had so quickly "adapted to school" and made "new, Christian friends." I'm sure you can guess what happened.

The problem was that Liz' mom had focused on the externals. She was concerned solely with Liz' behavior. Linda had not taken the time to look deeper. She was a busy career woman, paying the school to fix her daughter's problem.

Liz and her newfound friend, Brenda, were creative in their defiance. They dyed their hair; they wore clothes that were outside the rules of the school; and looked like they had shopped at "Street Walkers R Us."

After a few weeks, Liz was suspended for coming to school drunk. Her mom was upset, but she blamed Brenda.

What was wrong with this mom? She thought environment determined choice. Linda believed her daughter was not able to make good decisions on her own. Bottom line: she didn't trust Liz. Maybe she shouldn't; she had not prepared Liz to make wise decisions on her own.

We can't always be with our kids. Now that they are teens we don't want to! So, how can we influence them when we are away from them?

MOVING FROM CONTROL TO INFLUENCE

I believe one of the critical first steps is realizing *we can't control teenagers.*

When they were younger, we could control them. They were with us most of the time. But as teenagers, they are away from us hours at a time. How can we make sure they are being good?

Give up the notion that you can control your teen when she is away from you. Instead, try to approach your teen from a position of influence.

In other words, switch your position from control to influence. This is critical for parents of teenagers. What works with nine year olds does not work as well with fourteen year olds. Why is that?

With younger children we can take a position of direct

and firm control: "Don't put the Legos in the toilet, or I'll take them away from you." With younger children, we assumed responsibility for initiating punishment. We tried to control our precious child with rules and swift punishment for misbehavior. Generally, it worked.

But now, as our child becomes older, threats of taking away the Legos blocks don't seem to carry the same impact. The control position doesn't work as well as our children get older.

But some of us still try to control our teen.

Why?

I think it could be because we are focusing on our teen's behavior. We are focusing on the externals. Take Liz, for instance; her mom focused on her behavior, not her internals. She didn't take time to understand how Liz felt and what she was thinking. Besides, she didn't trust her anyway. "She just needs to change her behavior and friends."

What *will* motivate our teens to make wise decisions?

I believe teens will be motivated to make wise decisions if we focus on developing their internal qualities, not simply their behavior. The externals have to do with performance and status. The internals have to do with character, integrity, initiative, and other virtues.

Unfortunately, we parents tend to focus on externals in our own lives: success at work, an active social calendar, and belonging to several clubs or groups. Our activities and duties often limit our times with the family, and we can begin to view our children as objects instead of people. In trying to handle our stress as employees and parents, "we can treat people as simplistic stereotypes" and our own children "as objects or symbols—not as full subjects . . ." argues psychologist David Elkind. He explains why:

> Parents under stress see their children as symbols because it is the least demanding way to deal with them. A student, a skater, a tennis player, a confidant are clear-cut symbols, easy guides for what to think, to see, and how to behave. Symbols

thus free the parent from the energy consuming task of knowing the child as a totality, a whole person.[1]

Liz' mom was under stress. She saw Liz as an object or symbol. A symbol that needed changing. Looking at our teens as caricatures reduces them to a pattern of behaviors. This makes it easier for the parents to deal with their teens, because parents are looking at them as a stereotype. "It is the least demanding way to deal with them," Elkind declares. It is also the least effective.

Liz' mom was guilty of "drive-by parenting." She only took time to glance at her daughter. She didn't take time to really know her. She only knew a caricature of Liz.

Stressed and hurried parents tend to focus only on what they see. As a result, they often raise defiant kids. The kids don't feel cared for. They are reacting to being treated as objects. Speaker and author Ken Davis suggests a better approach:

> Our goal as parents . . . is not just to change our children's outward behavior; we also need to affect their inner commitment to principle, the values that govern the way they see themselves and the world. If we're successful in that, we effect change from the inside out. The child who has a personal commitment not to drink because of his personal value system will be strong in resisting outside pressure.[2]

INTERNAL VERSUS EXTERNAL STANDARDS

As parents of teenagers, we can become obsessed with the externals: "You aren't old enough to wear makeup," "You aren't going out of the house looking like that!" "You can't date until you are sixteen," or "Your first year of dating will be double-dating with us." (Can you tell I am an anxious father of two teenage girls?)

Rules like these don't create an inner commitment to principle within the teenager. They are external and parent-oriented. In other words, they will probably fail.

Make It an Internal Issue

Make it an internal issue. The statement "You must demonstrate modesty in how you dress" points to an attitude, not an action. Similarly you can require thoughtful treatment of another's possessions by making it an inner issue: "You need to show respect for others by how you treat their property."

I often speak to high school students. Invariably, I am asked, "When is a teen ready to date?" Here is what I tell them: "You are ready to date when you understand the benefits of dating, the dangers of dating, your standards for dating; and have committed to write them and live them."

This is the teen's personal dating agreement. It is a covenant she makes with herself and shares with her parents. In essence, she is saying, "This is what I believe about dating and what I am committed to do."

When it's all said and done, our teens are going to make their decisions based on *their* values, not *ours*. We want to shape those values before the heat of the moment. Our ambition is to develop inner conviction.

When a teen has taken time to think seriously about dating, is aware of the dangers and benefits, and is committed to predetermined moral standards, then he or she is ready to date. I have seen fourteen year olds who have been able to do this and I have seen nineteen year olds who couldn't. My preference is to put the teen to the test rather than allow them to date at the magical age of sixteen.

My fear has been that parents will say, "No dating until you're sixteen," but not prepare their teen for dating. Their teen then begins dating without any preparation or inner commitment to principles. It is a recipe for disaster.

As a responsible parent, you want to develop integrity and initiative. You're seeking compassion, not selfishness. The ultimate goal is to grow character, not conformity. When we do this, we help our teens stand alone. We empower them to make decisions based on principle, not popularity or pressure.

A character-based approach will help your teen make wise decisions even if she is away from you.

When I speak to teenage audiences, one of my favorite Scriptures to speak on is Jeremiah 9:23–24: "This is what the Lord says: 'Let not the wise man boast of his wisdom or the strong man boast of his strength or the rich man boast of his riches, but let him who boasts boast about this: that he understands and knows me, that I am the Lord, who exercises kindness, justice and righteousness on earth, for in these I delight,' declares the Lord."

This powerful Scripture contains some tools that will empower teens to make good decisions—decisions they can be proud of, decisions that will help them develop a solid, permanent self-worth.

Our culture tells us that to feel good about ourselves we need beauty, brains, and bucks. But God's Word offers a refreshing approach that is true, time-tested, and developed by our Creator. In this Scripture, we discover that biblical self-worth comes from:

1. Knowing and understanding God
2. Experiencing God's kindness and grace
3. Experiencing God's forgiveness and justice
4. A growing desire to do the right thing (righteousness)
5. Realizing that the first four things delight God

We want our teenagers to base their worth as a person on what God says, rather than what others think. There is a lot of pressure for teens to be popular and cool. Those pressures don't change much when we become adults. We all want to be liked. Help your teen understand that the bottom line is that *God is more concerned with your character than your popularity.*

The following chart contrasts the difference between popularity and character as a foundation for your teen's self-worth.

Chart 9
A TEEN'S CHOICE:
POPULARITY OR CHARACTER[3]

Popularity (Cool Reputation)	Character
Goal: to be liked	Goal: to be like Christ
Focus: What I do	Focus: Who I am
Depends on others' thoughts	Not interested in public opinion
Something you have to strive to earn and achieve	Given to you by God
Exclusive—only for the popular people	Anyone can have it
Can be gained or lost quickly	Achieved through a slow process of growth; cannot be taken away
Causes people to play the fool to maintain	Not dependent on success
God may take reputation away to build character	God will not take character away to build a popular reputation
Afraid of adversity	Survives adversity

Most of us have discovered what teenagers will learn later. Beauty will fade with time. Brains might get you good grades in school, but they don't guarantee that you will make wise decisions. Bucks will buy you stuff, but those things can't promise lasting happiness. Beauty, brains, and bucks are the pursuits of our culture. If our teens chase after them, they will be fragile and susceptible to the winds of the culture. Our challenge is to build into our teens a commitment to inner principle—a desire to build character. Then they will be able to resist the short-term diversions and pursue values and virtues that are lasting and commendable.

BUILDING CHARACTER: THE FRAMEWORK FOR WISE DECISIONS

Helping our teens to make wise decisions on their own will lead to trust and intimacy in our relationship with them. They will feel that we trust them and have prepared them to make their own decisions. This removes some of the "power play" aspects that are common in parent-teen relationships. When trust is evident in a parent-teen relationship, there can be closeness. This can really pay off for teens when they face temptation.

Researchers Merton and Irene Strommen found that teens who had affectionate and caring parents resisted negative behaviors better and were freer to develop as individuals than their peers. Specifically,

> There is significantly less social alienation among adolescents whose parents emphasize nurturance, as well as less involvement in drug or alcohol use and sexual activity. In nurturing homes we find more adolescents who know how to make friends and maintain good relationships with them; more who are involved in helping-type behaviors and more who tend to view religion as a liberating and challenging force in their lives.[4]

What does it mean to build our teens' internal qualities? It means to prepare them for life, from the inside out.

It's more than teaching them rules. It's more than passing on family values. It's about developing our teen's inner commitment to principle. When we motivate our teens inwardly, we shape their character—and we will motivate them to good and noble outward behavior.

Scripture teaches that wisdom is acquired through daily opportunities. We can't count on a class, a book, or a sermon. Wisdom is best passed on as we *walk* through life (Deuteronomy 6:7). A wise parent seizes the opportunities that life presents to teach principles which help shape character. A wise parent takes the initiative.

Consider the words of Daniel Hahn, author and pastor to students and families:

What can a parent do about it? we cry. But if we're honest, most of us will confess that while we hide behind a scarcity of "ideas" what we really lack is action. The real problem isn't what we *can* do but what we *will* do.

- Will we sit down and talk with our children after school and find out exactly what they're picking up?
- Will we take the time to write letters and make phone calls when legislation is being considered that affects what happens in our schools and homes?
- Will we move the couch in front of the TV— in order to block the view, not to improve it—and take back that position of influence in our home?
- Will we listen or read the lyrics our kids are listening to and use them as a springboard for discussion?
- Will we set real and firm boundaries about appropriate media entertainment, and live out that standard in front of our kids?
- Will we supplant some of what is being beamed into our households with relevant conversations based on God's Word and God's principles for life?
- Will we make our child's "Christian education" as important as their "intellectual education"?[5]

RESPONSE-ABILITY

A Classic Definition

Our goal is to prepare our teens for life. How do we do it?

When I teach my parenting seminars, I often display a definition: "Responsibility is being willing to be held accountable for your behavior."

I ask the parents, "Where have you heard this definition used?"

"At work."

"In the military."

"By my parents."

I ask, "What is missing from this definition?"

Some people can see it right away. Teenagers always spot it. They are always asking, "What's in it for me?"

Responsibility is being willing to be held accountable for your behavior.

This classic definition of responsibility doesn't address the "what's in it for me?" question. It creates a picture of someone in authority checking on you. You will do your job as long as they are looking. The emphasis is on their observing you. As a result, the definition is condescending and seems punitive.

It's not very motivating.

A New Definition

Let me introduce you to a new definition for the same word:

Response-Ability is being prepared to take on life's situations.

We want our teens to be prepared to take on life's situations. We want them to look to the future with confidence and capability. We want them to be committed to internal principles and not swayed by changing popular opinion.

The classic definition of "responsibility" focuses on the past and on external behavior. The revised definition focuses on the future and deals with the whole person, internally and externally. It motivates teens because it empowers them to shape their future by being prepared to make wise decisions. And wise decisions, according to Solomon, have surpassing value: "Blessed is the man who finds wisdom, the man who gains understanding, for she is more profitable than silver and yields better returns than gold. She is more precious than rubies; nothing you desire can compare with her" (Proverbs 3:13–15).

A CONVERSATION ABOUT RESPONSE-ABILITY

Help your teen prepare for life by helping her understand this fresh definition. Try having a conversation something like this:

"Do you have a few minutes to talk?"

"Sure, Dad. What's up?"

"Do you mind turning down your CD player so we can hear each other?"

"No problem. It was only on 3."

"Who was that, anyway?"

"That's the latest from the Smashed Nocturnal Rodents. Cool, huh?"

"Well . . . Hey, the reason I wanted to talk is I want to be a better parent."

"Excuse me?" she gasps in shock.

"Yeah, that's right. I want to be a better parent. I want to be more trusting of you. In fact, I want to work myself out of a job. Are you interested in helping me?"

"Will it affect my allowance?"

"Not negatively."

"Sure—count me in," your teenage daughter says.

"I want to work myself out of the job of always telling you what to do and how to behave. I want to help you become more independent. My goal is to prepare you to take on life's situations."

"Huh? Whadya say, Dad?"

"I said, I'd like to help you do more so I can do less. Less telling. Less nagging."

"What?! What was the part about less nagging?"

"That's right, less nagging. I turn over more and more areas to you, and you demonstrate that you can make wise choices. I nag less and worry less."

"All right. What do I do?"

"Just answer a few questions. Be as honest as you can."

"OK." Your daughter stares at you out of the corner of her eye.

"What do I do that makes you feel like an adult?"

"Oh, that's easy, Dad. I feel like an adult when you trust me to go out past midnight with my friends."

"You mean the negotiable curfew idea."

"Yeah. I don't like a rigid curfew like some of my friends have. If I need to stay out later, you let me negotiate."

"Well, that's when you really have something to do, not just to 'hang out.'"

"Yeah, I know. You seem reasonable with that. It makes me feel like an adult."

"OK, thanks. Now, here is the next question: What do I do that makes you feel like a child?"

"When you always ask if I need a coat when I am going out. I know how cold it is. I know when to bring a jacket or a sweater."

"All right. What is one area where you could use less direction from me?"

"Hmmm. Let me see . . . Oh, I know, I could use some more freedom and less direction from you about my homework. I'm doing fine. Getting good grades, mostly A's and B's. I can handle it."

"I see. How about an area you could use more input or direction from me?"

"Dad, I really want to get my driver's license. Will you take me out and show me the basics? I'm afraid to go to driver's school without a little road experience."

"Sure, we can do that. OK, daughter, one last question: Are you interested in learning how to take on life's situations? Can I coach you to prepare for some challenges I think you will encounter?"

"Yeah, sure, Dad."

"Great. Let's redefine a word. Let's make it our definition: *Response-Ability is being prepared to take on life's situations.* What do you think, daughter?"

"Sounds interesting. Can we get back to the part where you do less nagging and I get more freedom?"

HELPING YOUR TEEN MAKE WISE DECISIONS

Three Important Steps

We can prepare our teens to take on life and make wise decisions. To do this, we need to understand and implement three essential steps:

1. *Focus on building virtues that will last.* Earlier in this chapter I introduced three qualities that we would like to see built up in our teens: kindness, justice, and righteousness (Jeremiah 9:23–24). Try to define what these words mean to you. Ask yourself, *How can I nurture these virtues in my teen?* Spend time contrasting being cool with developing character. Discuss these contrasts with your teen.

2. *Discover and affirm the unique personality and gifts of your teenager.* Can you complete these statements? "My teen is unique because. . . ." "A unique gift he/she has is. . . ." If you have more than one child, you already know that children are different from each other. They will approach decision-making differently as well. If we can study and come to understand each teen's individual differences, it will help us as we coach them in this important life skill.

3. *Search for your teen's positive inner values and convictions, and focus on developing them.* Ask yourself: *What is one positive inner value my teen has? What can I do to reinforce and strengthen that value?* We hear a lot about "family values." But for many of us, we aren't sure how to pass on to our teens what is important to us. I believe we can empower our teens through values.

Decision-Making and Values

Parents can empower their teens through values when they identify and model them. It is true: Values are more caught than taught.

In his book, *Teaching Your Child to Make Decisions,* Gordon Porter Miller offers four practical skills in a process that helps parents pass on values to their teen: (1) translating values into goals; (2) clarifying and pursuing what is wanted (goals); (3) discovering and developing ways to reach goals; and (4) learning to assess the risks (consequences) involved in any action.[6]

I have modified Dr. Miller's skills into a step-by-step approach to decision-making:

Step One: Choose one value. (The value should be some quality you want to see developed in your teen.) For example, "I want my teen to learn to be compassionate and kind."

Step Two: Express this value as a goal. Put the goal in writing. For example, "He would be kind if he wouldn't beat up his brother and would be considerate toward him"; or "He would be compassionate if he served someone in need."

Step Three: Discuss with your teen the quality you want to see developed. Ask him if there are other examples he can think of that illustrate the desired quality in action.

Step Four: Decide together on a reasonable goal. What behavior would demonstrates the virtue in action? Make the goal measurable and reasonable. Be sure your teen agrees with the goal. Here are a couple of examples: "I will not beat up or harass my brother for a month." "As a family, we will serve at the rescue mission one Saturday each month."

Step Five: Assess the benefits and risks of the goal. What are the positive consequences of reaching the goal? For the teen who desires to not "beat up or hassle" his brother, the main benefit is obvious, and he can write it down: "I will not get in trouble for fighting with my brother." Also have him consider the risks. What are the negative consequences of not reaching the goal? "If I am unkind to my brother I will be required to serve him thirty minutes a day for a week. Some ways I might serve him include: doing his yard chores, washing his clothes, cleaning up his room, helping with his paper route, and washing dishes on his night."

In decision-making with teens it is important for the teen to consider "What are the benefits?" and "What are the risks?" This helps them understand the law of cause and effect.

It forces them to consider the consequences for the choices they make. Thus, step five is crucial.

Step Six: Allow your teen to make the decision and evaluate the results. As he evaluates the results, some questions he may ask are: "Did it turn out the way I planned? Were there benefits or risks that I wasn't anticipating?"

I have used the following chart to help teens make decisions. Make a copy of it and give it to your teen the next time he/she needs to make an important decision. It can act as a grid as he moves to a decision and later evaluates his action.

My Decision

The following seven items can outline the issues for your teen as he moves toward making a wise decision. Have him put his own responses on a sheet of paper as he personalizes his decision.

The Decision: *Should I play basketball another season?*
Options: *Yes—I hope to do better. No—I'll go out for swimming instead.*
Feelings: *I'd miss my friends from basketball camp.*
Risks: *Losing my shot, and my friends.*
Results: *I would be lonely and may not be that good at swimming, anyway.*
My Decision: *To play basketball one more season.*
Evaluation: (to be completed after the decision) *I'm glad I went out for basketball. We had a great season.*

By combining the step-by-step values transformation process with the "My Decision" tool, we can help our teens acquire the skills to make wise decisions.

Parents often underestimate their teens. Often a teen will know what he or she really wants to do, if only people would leave him or her alone. What your teen wants is usually in line with family values and traditions. Your teen needs your help; not in supplying answers and solutions, but in developing the skill to make wise decisions.

Teens are looking for support in processing the decision and following through once it is made. Our role is to provide support; agree on limits to be observed; and share our feelings and experience. Miller summarizes our role as parents in helping our teens make decisions:

> Make suggestions that will help your child decide. Keep an eye on actions and results so you can know when intervention may be necessary (when things are clearly beyond your child's control; when your child is clearly in danger). You can do all of that—and it can make a world of difference— without taking over your child's life. Think of yourself as something of a coach. *You can prepare the player for the game ahead, but you can't play and win it for him or her.*[7]

For "Almost Cool" Parents

1. Parents of teens need to switch their position from control to influence if they are to be effective. What, if anything, makes you uncomfortable with giving up control?
2. Have you observed parents seeing their teens as symbols? Discuss your thoughts about that.
3. How can a parent know if his teenager has internalized positive personal values?
4. Review Chart 9, "A Teen's Choice: Popularity or Character." Youth culture pulls on teens to be popular. What are some ways parents can help teens resist this pressure through an emphasis on building character?
5. Complete the following: "I know my teen will be making wise decisions when. . . ."

Chapter 12
GIVING AN EMOTIONAL AND SPIRITUAL LEGACY

I was excited to hear Phil's voice on the phone, elated that a former student in my youth group had called me. We talked about marriage and being in Bible school. And he thanked me for all "I learned from you when you were our youth pastor."

"Thanks Phil," I said. "What would you say made the most impact on you?"

"Actually, I can't think of any particular lesson that you taught. In fact, I can't remember *any* lesson that you taught."

Six years of listening to me speak two or three times a week, and you can't remember one lesson! I thought. "So my teaching made a huge impact," I suggested sarcastically.

"It wasn't your teaching that I will remember. It was when you let me come over and help you with the lawn work. It was when you let me take care of your yard and dog when you were on vacation. Also, it was meeting us for Tuesday Toast With Tim. I'll never forget those greasy breakfasts!"

I had imagined that my teaching or my leadership skills had made an indelible impact on Phil. He was one of our student leaders and now was preparing for a youth ministry career. But it wasn't my creative teaching or my leadership savvy that influenced Phil; it was my relationship with him.

Phil's words taught me an important lesson. Teens are more influenced by our relationship than by our lessons. Our goal as parents is to influence our teens. We want to make an impact.

We have a choice about what kind of impact we make on our teens. As I see it, we can leave a legacy or a lunacy. We know what kinds of lunacy are often passed on: addictions, craziness, dysfunction, and alienation. We are too familiar with the lunacy that can continue from generation to generation. But what about a legacy?

A *legacy* is an emotional and spiritual inheritance. It is a gift passed from one generation to the next.

A BLESSING

I once told a group of parents, some of whom were quite wealthy, "Your children can outspend or outlive any financial inheritance you may leave them."

Several heads nodded in agreement.

"Your children can ruin the family name. They can wipe out a financial inheritance or a social inheritance; but they won't destroy an emotional and spiritual inheritance. An emotional and spiritual inheritance outlives you more than any other kind of inheritance. It equips your children to take on life. It empowers them for years after you are gone. A legacy is a spiritual inheritance."

Now everyone was listening attentively.

Choosing the Blessing

"Remember the TV game show *Let's Make a Deal?*" I continued. "On it they had Door Number One and Door Number Two. Well, we have a similar choice. Which would you choose? Behind Door Number One, *blessing!* Behind Door Number Two, *cursing* (that's the lunacy). Which would you choose?"

On cue, my audience shouted, "Door Number One!"

"Right. We want to experience blessing. Consider this Scripture passage:

> You shall not make for yourself an idol in the form of anything in heaven above or on the earth beneath or in the waters below. You shall not bow down to them or worship them; for I, the Lord your God, am a jealous God, punishing the children for the sin of the fathers to the third and fourth generation of those who hate me, but showing love to thousands who love me and keep my commandments. (Deuteronomy 5:8–10)

"Do you know what that means? *The blessing is greater than the curse.* Isn't that good news? We might experience some form of generational sin or lunacy, but the good news of the gospel is that the blessing is greater than the curse."

The parents were smiling. Some of them looked like an eighty-pound backpack had been lifted from their shoulders.

"That's what grace is all about. A definition I like to use for *grace* is 'love in relationship.' God loved us so much that He didn't want anything to interfere with our relationship with Him; so He sent Jesus. He loves us that much. That's part of the blessing. What would you say is the curse?"

"Besides teenagers?" asked one witty father.

"Yes, what would you say is a curse?" I asked.

"Having to go through some painful experience?" ventured one mother.

"Yes, that's close. A curse is a divine judgment for breaking God's law. It results in natural consequences and punishment. A curse is a loss of freedom. For parents, it's the kids being out of school for the holidays. For students, their curse is having to return to school after the holidays. Think of a curse as losing something."

A woman in the back row raised her hand. "I hear the

word *blessing* used a lot, but I really don't know what it means. Could you tell us?"

"Sure. I am kind of like you. I am familiar with the word, but I didn't really understand it until recently. The word *blessing* means to kneel and show honor to another."

Placide's Blessing

Then I told the audience about Placide, who emigrated from Uganda and settled into a steady job in southern California.[1] One summer his mother-in-law came to visit from Uganda. She became seriously ill and had to be hospitalized. I found out and visited her. I enjoyed our conversation, prayed for her healing, and left. Later, I sent flowers and arranged for some meals to be brought to their home.

God answered our prayers. She recovered well enough to return to Uganda. She died a few weeks later.

Placide called and asked if he could stop by my office. When he arrived he asked me to sit in my chair. "I am going to offer you an African blessing. In Uganda when we want to say 'thank you' we bless someone. We show our honor and respect. This is how we show gratitude." He got on his knees and placed his hands on my knees. He smiled and prayed: "Thank You, God, for brother Tim. He has done so much for me, my family, and my mother-in-law. Thank You, God, for helping him to be there when we needed him. He is a faithful friend."

"I could tell that Placide was very serious," I told the audience. "This was a special moment. I was deeply moved. Maybe it was having my friend, who happens to be black, call me 'brother.' Maybe it was his words, or his hands touching my knees. He was in a humble position, down on his knees. He was demonstrating honor. I'm not sure which element was so powerful; probably the combination of all of these. But one thing is very clear to me: I received a blessing!"

"Then Placide continued. 'Father God, thank You for the compassion Tim has shown toward me and my family. Thank You for the love he showed Ellen during this difficult time. May You give him strength, health, and prosperity. Bless him in the way he blessed us. Amen.'

"Can you imagine how powerful that was for me?" I asked the alert crowd of parents. "I wasn't sure what to do, but I knew it was a treasured experience. A blessing can be very powerful."

THE FOCUS OF THE HEART

To give a blessing is to hope for power, success, fruitfulness, and longevity. It is a proclamation for a rich and abundant life. In contrast to a curse, which represents a loss, a blessing is an *addition of freedom and resources.*

If we want to pass on an emotional inheritance to our teens, we need to have a blessing on our heart. We all need The Blessing. Stephen Covey in *First Things First* says, "What most people want is to live, to love, to learn, and to leave a legacy."[2]

Most of us did not receive a blessing from our parents. How can we pass on something we didn't receive? I think part of the answer is learning to teach our teens to be principle-driven by using the natural instruction opportunities of life. We need to be prepared to teach the lessons that life hands us. What is on our heart is what we will pass on. The heart is the center of our will and emotions. Show me a person's passion, and I'll show you his heart.

A Focus on the Lord

The focus of our heart is very important. Is it on the Lord; are our faith and hope in Him? Our faith impacts our teens. Our faith can be a source of protection and refuge for our teens. "He who fears the Lord has a secure fortress, and for his children it will be a refuge" (Proverbs 14:26). They need to see that God is on our heart; that we have a reverence and awe (fear) of Him.

In Malachi 4:5–6, God declares that parents and children need to connect heart-to-heart about faith and other key issues, or the nation will suffer:

See, I will send you the prophet Elijah before that great and dreadful day of the Lord comes. He will turn the hearts of the fathers to their children, and the hearts of the children to their fathers; or else I will come and strike the land with a curse.

Why does He mention children? Why doesn't God say, "The most important thing is Bible study"? Or why doesn't He say, "Obey the Ten Commandments or I will curse your land."

Because *the church is only one generation away from extinction.* We need to pass faith on to our teens. We as parents —not the church youth group—are the primary source of spiritual growth for our kids. Listen to Moses' words about who teaches and leads children in the love of God.

Hear, O Israel: The Lord our God, the Lord is one. Love the Lord your God with all your heart and with all your soul and with all your strength. These commandments that I give you today are to be upon your hearts. Impress them on your children. Talk about them when you sit at home and when you walk along the road, when you lie down and when you get up. Tie them as symbols on your hands and bind them on your foreheads. Write them on the doorframes of your houses and on your gates. (Deuteronomy 6:4–9)

God's principles need to be impressed on our hearts first if we seek to pass them on to our children. The primary responsibility to pass on spiritual truth lies with the parents, not the church. The church's role is to equip parents to train their children.

The Last Word . . . and the First

Malachi 4:4–6 is God's last word. The last word is one of emphasis and importance. We pay attention to the final words of a loved one, whether spoken directly to us or written in a will. The Old Testament closed with these words. Before four hundred years of silence God wanted to have a dramatic last line; He declared, in essence, "Turn your hearts toward each other or suffer the consequences!"

God's last word in Malachi 4 was the importance of family and passing on the blessing from generation to generation.

Not only are the last words important, but the first words are, too. When we're "in love," we remember and fondly recall the first words said by the person who caught our attention. The first words we speak during a job interview can set the tone for the employer's attitude and follow-up questions.

In theology, the first words are important too. The Principle of First Mention says that the first time something is mentioned in Scripture it has special significance. We pay attention to the first words.

We know that His last words dealt with passing on the blessing from generation to generation. Do you know what His first words deal with in Matthew, the first book of the New Testament? Guess.

God's first words after four hundred years of silence were about *passing on the blessing from generation to generation.* Matthew 1 is the genealogy of Jesus. It is a record of His lineage from David and David's forebear, Abraham. It is a record of blessing from generation to generation.

If this subject is important enough to close the Old Testament and begin the New Testament, how important is it? Answer: *very important.*

I think God wanted us to get the point. The point is: We can pass on a blessing to our teens, if we choose to (and we really should!).

What will it take to turn our hearts? We need to focus our hearts on the things that matter. This means we will need to make a conscious decision to not focus on things that so easily demand our attention, but won't leave a legacy: work, sports, money, prestige, and things. This desire is to pass on a legacy that will outlive us. Fathers and mothers want to leave a lasting legacy. With God at the center, we can pass on a legacy of love and righteousness. As King David wrote, "From everlasting to everlasting, the Lord's love is with those who fear him, and his righteousness with their children's children—with those who keep his covenant and remember to obey his precepts" (Psalm 103:17–18).

WHAT KIDS WANT IN THEIR PARENTS

We want to connect with impact. We want to influence our teens to be people of faith. We want them to live lives that are pleasing to God.

How?

Let's first consider what teens want from their parents. One hundred thousand young teens were asked what they wanted most from their parents. The survey found the following top ten items on their list:

1. Parents who don't argue in front of them.
2. Parents who treat each family member the same.
3. Parents who are honest.
4. Parents who are tolerant of others.
5. Parents who welcome their friends into the home.
6. Parents who build a team spirit with their children.
7. Parents who answer their questions.
8. Parents who give punishment when needed, but not in front of others, especially their friends.
9. Parents who concentrate on good points instead of weaknesses.
10. Parents who are consistent.[3]

If we can have a relationship with our teens that is similar to this list, we will be able to connect heart-to-heart. We will be able to have the kind of relationship and environment that is conducive to passing on a legacy.

To help you understand how these basic issues help, consider the opposite of one. Let's say that you want to pass on your values to your teen but you don't know about number eight above: *Parents who give punishment when needed, but not in front of others, especially their friends.*

THE VAN RIDE

On the way home from practice with her son and his teammate, Meredith said, "Don't forget, you have youth group tonight. You need to get your homework done before you go."

"Oh, Mom! I have too much algebra. I can't get it done in time for youth group. Besides, I don't want to go—it's boring." He looks over to check the reaction of his teammate, who doesn't attend church.

"You're going and that's final!"

"Mom, I won't have time. I have forty equations to do and I—"

"Don't talk back to me! You need to learn respect. You can stay home this weekend. You are *grounded!*"

The teen looks at his friend with embarrassment, then mimics his mom for his friend's amusement.

What has Meredith accomplished?

She has forced her son to mimic her because she punished him in front of his friend—a cardinal sin for parents of teenagers. (His action is a humorous yet rebellious attempt to show his independence.) How will she be able to pass on values and help him develop virtues if she doesn't understand this principle?

Knowing what teens want will help us give them what they need.

SEVEN WAYS TO IMPACT YOUR CHILD'S FAITH

A legacy is an emotional and spiritual inheritance that you pass on to your child. It equips her to make wise decisions long after she has left home. The greatest spiritual legacy we can give is a lasting faith in Jesus Christ. How can we influence our teens to believe and grow in their trust and love of God and His Son, Jesus Christ? Here are seven ways to influence your teen's faith and to build a legacy.

1. Model a Growing and Personal Faith.

Deuteronomy 6:4–9 instructs parents to provide an example through the normal activities of the day: sitting, walking, lying down, and getting up. How we relate and behave in the natural flow of the day sends messages to our children. Our life is instructive, whether we intend for it to be or not. Dave Veerman, veteran youth worker and parent of teenagers, writes:

> Studies have consistently shown that children pick up the values of their parents. That is, they become most like their parents in how they live and where they invest their lives. Thus, the best way to instill in your teenagers a love for the church is to love the church yourself. This means making worship and Christian education a high priority in your lives, supporting your local church with your involvement and money, encouraging pastors and other church leaders, and consistently praying for your church.[4]

2. Include Faith in Normal Conversations.

What is on our heart will be on our lips. Does your teen hear you talk about spiritual issues? Do you integrate spiritual truth into your conversations about other topics. Or do you only talk about God on Sundays?

Take seriously the idea of discovering God in the ordinariness of life. We can discover the spiritual in the mundane, if we are willing to seek it.

Probably one of the most ordinary and frustrating routines for me is driving in Los Angeles traffic. It can be anxiety-producing. Recently we were traveling as a family in our van. A man in a speedy import changed lanes without signaling and cut me off. I braked quickly, averting an accident. The rude driver sped on without a clue that he had endangered our lives. I said, "That guy doesn't even know how close he was to hitting us. He is not a considerate driver."

"He must be in a hurry," said one daughter.

"He's a jerk. I hope he gets busted by the CHP," said the other daughter.

Seizing the moment, I said, "He is so wrapped up in his hurry to get somewhere he risked our lives, as well as others. I hope you girls will be considerate drivers when you start driving. Thank God He protected us. That was close."

It's not a sermon. It's not a parent-teen conference. It's integrating faith and values into a very normal conversation. Of course, I don't always respond that way when I am driving, but I'll leave those stories out!

3. Be Well-Rounded; Don't Compartmentalize Your Faith.

Some people are comfortable keeping God in a box. They relegate spiritual issues to a time and a place, with certain people. They don't allow their faith to infiltrate every aspect of their lives. When we compartmentalize our faith, our teens notice. They would say we aren't consistent. They might call us hypocrites. They would make excuses for themselves, why they believe one way and behave another. They would have learned it from their parents.

Your faith should influence your finances, how you spend your time, how you entertain, and how you relate. A growing and vital faith touches each aspect of our lives. When our teens see that our faith has infiltrated each area of our lives, they will perceive that it is very important to us; and therefore very important to them.

Jamie understands this principle. Her father, Jim, was a leader in the church. He was active on boards and eager to give speeches. At church he was known as an outgoing, dynamic leader.

"If people only knew what he was really like. He is such a goody-goody at church, but he is a selfish, impatient, and angry man at home," she told me.

I didn't believe her. I didn't know this side of her father. Before long, Jamie started to give her parents trouble. She came to my office to talk. "Why should I have to obey him? He's such a hypocrite! He tells me to study, work hard, and don't cheat, and he's out there rippin' people off!"

Jamie was furious. Her dad was asking her to live by ethical standards that he didn't follow. He would talk in "sweet syrupy spiritual language" around church and church people; but not live anything like that. "He needs to walk his talk," she told me.

As it turned out, she was right. Jim turned out to be a hypocrite. His faith did not influence his home or his business. Jim's greed and his lack of ethics landed him in jail and cost him his business. Jamie was one of the first to blow the whistle. Teens have a sensitivity to fairness, justice, and consistency.

4. Be Authentic.

Jim wasn't authentic. He was fake. Because of his duplicity, Jamie rejected her family's faith, and even her family. My hope for her is that she will discover authentic Christianity.

Teens are looking for the genuine article. They can sniff a phony. They aren't looking for perfection; they are looking for authenticity. A wise parent can be real and realistic because he has given up the notion of perfection. He has more energy to parent because he doesn't have to spend so much of it acting. Parents caught up in the performance trap tend to be fatigued and irritable. They also tend to be insecure because they are afraid that someday their "real self" might be exposed.

Walt Mueller, executive director of the Center for Parent/Youth Understanding, comments:

> Our gnawing sense of imperfection should not keep us from being good parents. Realistic parents pave the way for family closeness and build their children's self-esteem by parenting with grace. They aren't paralyzed by feelings of fear and inadequacy when they make mistakes. They know that since

the beginning of time, God has used imperfect people to carry out his plan, and he will use them as they raise their children in spite of their imperfections.[5]

5. Serve Together.

If values are more caught then taught, spend some time throwing values your teens will catch. Design some faith demonstrations. Discover ways you and your teen can serve together.

I discovered this principle when I was a youth pastor. I could lecture youth on compassion. We would discuss the importance of demonstrating love. I would have the teens read and memorize Scriptures about love and service. All of this work did not produce a loving and serving youth group. It wasn't until I started monthly service projects and regular missions trips that I began to see a change in my students. They learned to give to others and to love one another by serving together.

Do you want to know what is even more powerful? Having parents and teens serve together. I have seen parents who were alienated from their teens reconcile and reconnect because they built a house together for needy people. There is something very powerful about a family serving together.

Discuss with your teen what you could do together to demonstrate your faith. Tell him, "We are going to take our faith on the road. What should we do?"

Some suggestions: work in a soup kitchen or rescue mission, take clothes to the homeless, build a house for Habitat for Humanity, support a child in another country, have a garage sale and give the money to a charitable group, contact your local Crisis Pregnancy Center and ask how you can help, plan for a short-term foreign mission trip, and ask your church what projects need to be done.

6. Pray for Your Teens and with Them.

Parenting skills are important, but one of the most powerful tools a Christian parent has is prayer. When our teens know we are praying for them, it influences them. My friend Daniel Hahn describes the impact of prayer in his own life in *The Pro-Teen Parent:*

> My parents never followed me around, or (to my knowledge) ever snooped through my stuff or called others to check up on me. What they *did* do was hold a daily prayer vigil in my honor. They prayed about choices and friends and dates and driving habits. The knowledge of their prayers haunted me when temptations arose, and comforted me when the blows of adolescence hit hard. Their prayers were like a guardian angel that followed me day and night. Nothing could have given me a greater sense of their twenty-four-hour love and concern than to know their prayers were continuously ascending.[6]

Our prayers can protect and guide our teens. We should also pray with our teens. It doesn't need to be a sixty-minute prayer meeting. Just go in to "tuck them in" at night and ask, "What would you like me to pray about?" Sometimes they might want you to pray *with* them right then; at other times, they might want you to pray for them but not with them. Respect their wishes. Check back with them the next day or later to see how things are going. Let them know you were praying for their specific request.

Teenagers often equal anxiety. We worry about them. We need to pray for our teens for *our* sake. It will give us perspective and help us deal with our anxiety. As the apostle Paul wrote, we need not be anxious, only bring everything in prayer "with thanksgiving, present[ing] your requests to God" (Philippians 4:6). "Parents, we need to pray for answers—answers to the questions that we have about raising our children and answers to our children's adolescent questions and their deep spiritual longing for him," writes Mueller, who adds, "It is ultimately God who gives faith to our kids and leads them to spiritual health."[7]

7. Learn and Communicate Love in Their Language.

One of the most loving acts we can demonstrate to our teens is to introduce them to a personal and growing relationship with Christ. Parents can have a huge influence on their teen's faith by their example of love. In fact, most young adults attribute their acceptance of Christ as Savior to the loving influence of their parents.[8]

How do we communicate love to a teenager? If you are going to speak to the natives, you have to learn their language. Each teenager has a language of love. If you are speaking in another language, they won't understand your love.

Gary Chapman develops this theme for marriage in his excellent book *The Five Love Languages:*

> We have long known that in early childhood development each child develops unique emotional patterns. . . . Some children grow up feeling loved, wanted, and appreciated, yet others grow up feeling unloved, unwanted, and unappreciated.
>
> The children who feel loved by their parents and peers will develop a primary love language based on their unique psychological makeup and the way their parents and other significant persons expressed love to them. They will speak and understand one primary love language.[9]

Chapman has written specifically about parents learning to speak their children's particular love language in his sequel, *The Five Love Languages of Children*. The idea of speaking your child's primary love language certainly applies to parenting your teen. If you can discover and speak your teen's love language, he will have his emotional needs met and be able to develop into a responsible adult. You will have empowered your child with the blessing of an emotional and spiritual inheritance.

Here is a summary of the five love languages.[10]

1. *Words of Affirmation.* Words that are kind and encouraging will affirm your teen. Words express appreciation and value. Make a list of the things that you appreciate about your teen. For ideas on affirming words, consider the "Thirty Ways to Encourage Your Teen" on pages 128–30. Develop your own list and refer to it daily. Pass on at least one compliment to your teen each day. If your teen responds to affirming words, that may be her love language.

2. *Quality Time.* Quality time means giving your teen undivided and focused attention. It often means doing something that he enjoys. Many adults may not be able to remember what their parents *said* to them when they were teenagers, but they remember what they *did* with them. Showing interest in what our teens are interested in and being willing to participate in their interest communicates love.

Karen is interested in miniatures. Doll houses and tiny replicas of Victorian towns are her favorites. Her father, Ken, would rather be watching sports on TV. Ken knows this is her interest, so he gives up his Saturday game to take Karen to a Miniature Show at the County Fairgrounds. Karen's love language is quality time. She feels loved by her father. Ken is a wise father. There aren't too many opportunities to connect with a fourteen-year-old daughter. His choice communicates love.

3. *Receiving Gifts.* If your teen loves to give and receive gifts, his language of love may be receiving gifts. A teen who has this language will express gratitude to the giver, show others the gift, and make a big deal about it. He may spend a large part of his income buying gifts for friends and family. The cost of the gifts isn't as important as the thought and the emotion that it represents. A teen who thinks in this language will feel loved by the parent who stops on the way home from work and purchases the teen's favorite candy bar or magazine.

Some parents think this is the only love language teens understand. They may buy too many things for their teens only to discover that they don't seem to appreciate them. The parent may not be meeting the needs of the teen by giving gifts—this may not be their language. It could be that for those teens, their language is:

4. *Acts of Service.* When our teens were younger we were constantly serving them. Now, we serve them differently. We drive them places, take them shopping, cook for them, and help them with school projects. For some teens, this means a lot. For instance, you could choose a task that is particularly not appealing to your teen. Say, "I cleaned up the dog messes for you. I love you." Tell your teen that you love him/her when you do an act of service for him/her.

If your teen expresses gratitude for your acts of service, it could be an indicator that this is her language of love. If you aren't sure which language of love your teen understands, observe her. See how she expresses love to others. That is a clue to her love language.

5. *Physical Touch.* Teens still need to feel their parents' affection through appropriate touch. Physical touch can be very powerful. It may be our first love language. Long before we can understand words or speak we can understand love through touch.

Physical touch is very important to all children and teens, even those whose primary love language is not physical touch.

Michelle is recovering from her boyfriend's breaking up with her. Her friends have said words of encouragement and spent time trying to get her mind off of Jason. But what really seems to help is her parents sitting close to her and letting her rest her head on a shoulder while they watch TV. She may be sixteen, but she still needs her parents' touch; especially now.

Study your children. Each child is different. What works with one may not work with another. What communicates love to your teen may not to her sibling.

There are many teens who have hearts that are empty. They feel that they have been cursed, not blessed. We must learn to speak our teen's language if we want them to feel loved.

I know of many parents who have put much effort into loving their teens, but their teens don't seem to respond. I ask them, "Could it be that you are loving them in a language they don't understand or value?" If they were to invest their effort into their teen's language of love I think they would see a satisfying response.

Become a student of your teenager. As you discover her primary love language, try speaking it daily. But do not neglect the other four. The secondary love languages will become more meaningful once you are speaking your teen's primary language.

THE BATON PASS

I coach track and field for our local club. I train my athletes to focus on the essentials. "Don't forget the basics!" When it comes to a relay, one of the basics is passing the baton. One of the worst things that can happen in a relay is to drop the baton. To avoid this, we practice handing off the baton. We work on stride, rhythm, signals, and movement, all crucial to a good baton pass. In a way, it's a dance. We have competed against teams who had faster runners, but who dropped the baton. We won the race.

Life is a relay. It doesn't matter what you start with. It's how you finish. You may start with natural abilities. You have a head start. But if you don't hand off well, what does it matter?

As parents, we want to hand off the baton to our teens. We want them to run well. We want them to finish. We want to pass on the baton of a legacy. We want to empower them to continue the race knowing we love them and have blessed them. We believe in them, and they know it. They can take the baton of an emotional and spiritual inheritance and run with confidence.

The family is God's primary institution for passing on the truth of His Word from one generation to another. The implication is quite clear. When parents stop passing on a godly legacy to their teens, a nation suffers. Societies are influenced one family at a time.

God has chosen to do His work through the family. It has proven to be the primary arena of bringing people to Himself. His plan is for parents to pass on the baton of spiritual truth to their teens.

When I was growing up in Colorado, one of my favorite places to visit was Central City. It was a rowdy cowboy town in the previous century. Visiting the cemetery, I enjoyed reading the tombstones. There were hustlers, rustlers, and common folk buried there. Their epitaphs were phrases that tried to say in a few words what a person's life had been like for decades.

But true epitaphs aren't etched on granite—they are carved on the hearts of our children, now teenagers. The last words on our lives will come from those we leave behind. God has placed teens in our lives as gifts. Gifts we are to influence and send into the next era, with our blessing.

For "Almost Cool" Parents

1. What comes to mind when you hear of an "emotional and spiritual inheritance"?
2. If "the church is only one generation from extinction," it is critical that parents pass on a vibrant faith to their teens. What are some creative ways you have heard of parents showing their faith to their children?
3. Read again the section "What Kids Want in Their Parents." If God is a heavenly Father, how does He demonstrate the qualities of fairness, honesty, and love exemplified in the Top Ten list on page 200?
4. Review the "Seven Ways to Impact Your Teen's Faith." Were any of these influential in your own spiritual development? What parent or spiritual mentor lived out one or more of these in front of you?
5. What do you think is your teen's language of love?

NOTES

Chapter 1: Understanding Their World

1. Dianne Hales, "How Teenagers See Things," *Parade*, 18 August 1996, 4.
2. Ibid.
3. Ibid., 4–5.
4. David Elkind, *All Grown Up and No Place to Go* (Reading, Mass.: Addison-Wesley, 1984), 179.
5. Mary Pipher, *Reviving Ophelia: Saving the Selves of Adolescent Girls* (New York: Ballantine, 1995), 81.
6. Victor Strasburger, *Getting Your Kids to Say "No" in the 90's When You Said "Yes" in the 60's* (New York: Fireside, 1993), 27.

Chapter 2: Understand Your Teen

1. Laurence Steinberg, quoted in *Youthworker Update* (El Cajon, Calif.: Youth Specialties Publications), 15 August 1991, 6.
2. Ibid.
3. Ibid. Also see Laurence Steinberg with B. Bradford Brown and Sanford M. Dornbusch, *Beyond the Classroom* (New York: Simon & Schuster, 1996), 102–3, 124–26. The book reports the findings of a twenty-year study of representative high school students in California and Wisconsin. Steinberg and his colleagues found that a parent's example, support of learning, and involvement in the child's school life benefited the child's success in school.
4. Dianne Hales, "The Mood of American Youth," *Parade* , 18 August 1996, 5.

5. Ibid.

6. Adapted from Teresa A. Langston, *Parenting Without Pressure* (Colorado Springs: NavPress, 1994), 83.

7. Charles Bradshaw, *You and Your Teen* (Elgin, Ill.: Cook, 1985), 11.

8. James E. Gardner, *Understanding, Helping, Surviving the Turbulent Teens*, (San Diego: Oak Tree, 1982), 181.

9. Stephen R. Covey, *First Things First* (New York: Simon & Schuster, 1994), 213.

10. Ross Campbell, *How to Really Love Your Teenager* (Wheaton, Ill.: Victor, 1985), 25.

11. Adapted from Langston, *Parenting Without Pressure*; 84.

Chapter 3: Change Your Parenting Perspective

1. Fred Gosman, *Spoiled Rotten* (New York: Villard, 1992) 206.

2. David Elkind, *All Grown Up and No Place to Go* (Reading, Mass.: Addison-Wesley, 1984), 13.

3. David Rice, *Parents in Control* (Eugene, Oreg.: Harvest House, 1987), 16.

4. John Rosemond, "Family Counselor," *Albuquerque Journal*, 24 April 1991, 8.

5. Bruno Bettelheim, *A Good Enough Parent* (New York: Knopf, 1987), 99.

Chapter 4: Your Teen's Character: A Matter of Balance

1. Ken Davis, *How to Live with Your Kids When You've Already Lost Your Mind* (Grand Rapids: Zondervan, 1992), 89.

2. Wes Haystead, *The 3,000 Year Old Guide to Parenting* (Ventura, Calif.: Regal, 1991), 95.

3. Quoted in Zig Ziglar, *Raising Positive Kids in a Negative World* (New York: Ballantine, 1989), 42.

4. Daniel Hahn, *Teaching Your Kids the Truth About Consequences* (Minneapolis: Bethany, 1995) 21.

5. Ibid., 23.

6. These steps in developing logical consequences also work well for younger children. A more detailed discussion of these steps, used with children, appears in my book *The Relaxed Parent* (Chicago: Northfield, 1996), 183–85.

Chapter 5: Talking with Your Teen

1. Haim Ginott, *Between Parent and Teenager* (New York: Avon Books, 1982), 23.

2. H. Stephen Glenn and Jane Nelsen, *Raising Self-Reliant Children in a Self-Indulgent World* (Rocklin, Calif.: Prima, 1988), 90–91.

3. William L. Coleman, *What Makes Your Teen Tick?* (Minneapolis: Bethany, 1993), 49.

4. Glenn and Nelsen, *Raising Self-Reliant Children*, 106, 112.
5. Coleman, *What Makes Your Teen Tick?*, 48.
6. Ibid., 47.

Chapter 6: Handling the Hormone Hurricane

1. Barry and Carol St. Clair, *Talking with Your Kids About Love, Sex and Dating* (San Bernardino, Calif.: Here's Life, 1989), 13–14.
2. Walt Mueller, *Understanding Today's Youth Culture* (Wheaton, Ill.: Tyndale, 1994), 224.
3. Sharon D. White and Richard R. DeBlassie, "Adolescent Sexual Behavior," *Adolescence* 27 (Spring 1992): 189; as quoted in Mueller, *Understanding Today's Youth Culture*, 224.
4. "Where Christians Learn," in Thom Schultz, *Youth Ministry Resource Book* (Loveland, Colo.: Group, 1988), 52.
5. Victor Strasburger, *Getting Your Kids to Say "No" in the 90's When You Said "Yes" in the 60's* (New York: Fireside, 1993), 99.
6. Merton P. Strommen and A. Irene Strommen, *Five Cries of Parents* (New York: Harper & Row, 1985), 72.

Chapter 7: Talking About Love, Sex, and Dating

1. Associated Press, "High School Sexuality," (Thousand Oaks, Calif.) *News Chronicle*, 4 January 1992, A–4.
2. Scott Talley, *Talking with Your Kids About the Birds and the Bees* (Ventura, Calif.: Regal, 1990), 139.
3. Barry and Carol St. Clair, *Talking with Your Kids About Love, Sex and Dating* (San Bernardino, Calif.: Here's Life, 1989), 56.
4. George Barna, *Today's Teens: A Generation in Transition*, 1991 report from the Barna Research Group (Glendale, Calif.), 8.

Chapter 8: Empowering Your Teen: Right Values and Encouragement

1. Gordon Porter Miller, *Teaching Your Child to Make Decisions* (New York: Harper and Row, 1984), 248–49
2. H. Norm Wright, *The Power of a Parent's Words* (Ventura, Calif.: Regal, 1991), 42.
3. Jack O. Balswick and Judith K. Balswick, *The Family* (Grand Rapids: Baker, 1979), 22–23.
4. William L. Coleman, *What Makes Your Teen Tick?* (Minneapolis: Bethany, 1993), 55–56.
5. Ibid., 56, emphasis added.
6. These tips for motivating teenage children are adapted from *The Relaxed Parent* (Chicago: Northfield, 1996), 155–62.
7. Ken Davis, *How to Live with Your Kids When You Have Already Lost Your Mind* (Grand Rapids: Zondervan, 1992), 126.

Chapter 9: Dealing With an Angry Teen

1. Ken Davis, *How to Live with Your Kids When You've Already Lost Your Mind* (Grand Rapids: Zondervan, 1992), 69.
2. Ross Campbell, *How to Really Love Your Teenager* (Wheaton, Ill.: Victor, 1981), 60.
3. Adapted from William Cutler and Richard Peace, *Parenting Adolescents* (Littleton, Colo.: Serendipity House, 1990), 38–39.
4. William L. Coleman, *What Makes Your Teen Tick?* (Minneapolis: Bethany, 1993), 109–10.
5. Ibid., 110.
6. G. Richard Louv, *Childhood's Future* (Boston: Houghton Miflin, 1990), 19.
7. The discussion of four levels of anger is adapted from Campbell, *How to Really Love Your Teenager*, 67–68.

Chapter 10: Dealing with a Hurting Teen

1. Jim Burns, *Surviving Adolescence* (Dallas: Word, 1990), 126; emphasis added.
2. Dave Veerman, *Parenting Passages* (Wheaton, Ill.: Tyndale, 1994), 119.
3. Victor Strasburger, *Getting Your Kids to Say "No'" in the 90's When You Said "Yes" in the 60's* (New York: Fireside, 1993), 164.
4. Stephen Arterburn and Jim Burns, *Drug-Proof Your Kids* (Pomona, Calif.: Focus on the Family, 1989), 16.
5. Adapted from Arterburn and Burns, *Drug-Proof Your Kids*, 19.
6. The SADD "Contract for Life" is reproduced from Students Against Driving Drunk, Marlboro, Mass. Used by permission.
7. Centers for Disease Control, February 1991 report, Atlanta, Ga., as quoted in Strasburger, *Getting Your Kids to Say "No,"* 130.
8. David R. Veerman, *Ozzie & Harriet Had a Scriptwriter*, (Wheaton, Ill.: Tyndale, 1996), 251.

Chapter 11: Helping Teens Make Wise Decisions

1. David Elkind, *The Hurried Child* (Reading, Mass.: Addison-Wesley, 1989), 28–29.
2. Ken Davis, *How to Live with Your Kids When You've Already Lost Your Mind* (Grand Rapids: Zondervan, 1992), 111.
3. Adapted from Tim Smith, *Letters to Nicole* (Wheaton, Ill.: Tyndale, 1995), 117.
4. Merton and Irene Strommen, *Five Cries of Parents* (San Francisco: Harper and Row, 1985), 94–95.
5. Daniel Hahn, *Teaching Your Kids the Truth About Consequences* (Minneapolis: Bethany, 1995), 38–39.
6. Adapted from Gordon Porter Miller, *Teaching Your Child to Make Decisions* (New York: Harper and Row, 1984), 227.
7. Ibid., 222; emphasis added.

Chapter 12: Giving an Emotional and Spiritual Legacy

1. Placide's story is also told in my book *The Relaxed Parent* on pages 197–98.

2. Stephen R. Covey, A. Roger Merrill and Rebecca R. Merrill, *First Things First* (New York: Fireside, 1994), 198.

3. Walt Mueller, *Understanding Today's Youth Culture* (Wheaton, Ill.: Tyndale, 1994), 340.

4. David R. Veerman, *Ozzie & Harriet Had a Scriptwriter* (Wheaton, Ill.: Tyndale, 1996), 78.

5. Mueller, *Understanding Today's Youth Culture*, 337.

6. Daniel M. Hahn, *The Pro-Teen Parent: The Ten Best Ways to Cheer on Your Teen's Growth* (Sisters, Oreg.: Questar, 1992), 100.

7. Mueller, *Understanding Today's Youth Culture*, 339.

8. In a survey of 710 teenagers, conducted by the Barna Research Group; 54 percent said that the key influence to their accepting Christ was their parents. See George Barna, *Today's Teens: A Generation in Transition*, 1991 report from the Barna Research Group (Glendale, Calif.), 39–40.

9. Gary Chapman, *The Five Love Languages* (Chicago: Northfield, 1995), 15–16.

10. For a detailed discussion, see Gary Chapman and Ross Campbell, *The Five Love Languages of Children* (Chicago: Northfield, 1997), 27–28, 31–95. See also Chapman, *The Five Love Languages*, 164–70.

A pastor and author, Tim Smith also leads seminars for parents of teens. For information about upcoming seminars, retreats, speaking engagements, or consulting services, please contact Tim at:

Wordsmith Communications
P.O. Box 7736
Thousand Oaks, CA 91359-7739

Include your name, address, telephone number or fax number with your specific request. You may also reach Tim via the Internet at TdWrdsmith@aol.com.

Moody Press, a ministry of Moody Bible Institute,
is designed for education, evangelization, and edification.
If we may assist you in knowing more about Christ
and the Christian life, please write us without obligation:
Moody Press, c/o MLM, Chicago, Illinois 60610.